The Life and Times of

MADAM BHIKAJI CAMA

The Life and Times of MADAM BHIKAJI CAMA

Rachna Bhola 'Yamini'

Ocean Books Pvt. Ltd.

ISO 9001:2008 Publishers

Published by
Ocean Books (P) Ltd.
4/19 Asaf Ali Road,
New Delhi-110 002 (INDIA)
e-mail: info@oceanbooks.in

ISBN 978-81-8430-366-7
The Life and Times of
MADAM BHIKAJI CAMA
by Rachna Bhola 'Yamini'

Edition
2018

Price
₹ 400.00 (Rupees Four Hundred only)

Printed at
S.B.M. Industries Pvt. Ltd., Rai (Har.)

To those for whom
the words like patriotism,
loyalty, faith, duty and self-sacrifice
are not mere etymological terms,
but empirical truths of life.

Author's Note

Madam Bhikaji Rustam Cama, better known as Madam Cama, has been a patroness and source of inspiration for the Indian revolutionaries in true sense of the term. She was the first Indian woman to struggle against the British rule for India's freedom.

It was she who accomplished the historical task of hoisting India's national flag at an international forum. She had played a major role in the revolutionary organisations formed for the freedom struggle in England and France in the beginning of the twentieth century.

The remarkable achievements during the life of Madam Cama comprise the revelation of the actual prevailing conditions in repressing India under the foreign rule, rendering every possible assistance to Indian revolutionaries, undertaking propaganda for nationalism through newspapers, getting support of revolutionaries from other countries, promoting and distributing secret revolutionary literature, making arrangements for transport of arms and ammunition from foreign countries, and the like.

The daughter and daughter-in-law of an affluent family, Madam Cama had to face expulsion from the country only because she wanted to see her country independent; she wanted to root out the oppressive and atrocious British rule from India. She wanted to establish a republic which could stand straight before the whole world proudly and gloriously.

Madam Cama had to pass thirty-five years of her life abroad in exile. She was not allowed to return to India. Such a mighty British empire was frightened of this lady who had been termed as a dangerous and aggressive revolutionary. The memory of Mother India never dimmed in her mind even when she was abroad. The sole goal of her life was the realization of freedom for the country.

She became the harbinger of revolution and shared the pleasures and sorrows of the revolutionaries. She inspired and initiated every Indian youth in patriotism. Not only this, she sacrificed her private property, pleasure and comfort for the cause of her motherland. She was isolated from her home and family completely; her relation with her relatives had been cut off, yet she was cursed by these, solitary sojourn proved a boon for her. Had she been in India, family and social limitations and opposition by the English government could not have allowed her to implement her ideas. On the foreign soil, she worked for the country's freedom using all her strength.

Taking pride in the culture and traditions of her country, Madam Cama abided by her religious beliefs and traditions throughout her life, she brought into practice the teachings and tenets of Parsi faith in her life. She also taught the Indian youths studying abroad that they must not forget their own language, culture and civilization wherever they might go or live.

Though major part of her life was spent in foreign countries, yet Madam Cama continued to play a leading role amongst all revolutionary women of the Indian freedom struggle. Her ideology and principles continued to awake public consciousness. Once she determined her goal with the hailing of Vande Mataram, she did not allow herself to falter from this path.

This book has been written as a tribute to this great revolutionary: Madam Cama; regrettably who has been almost forgotten by the countrymen. This biography will be able to let the readers know about her life, mission and activities.

With this anticipation.

—Rachna Bhola 'Yamini'

Contents

1

Parsi Community and Madam Cama

Madam Bhikaji Rustam Cama belonged to the Parsi community. Despite she spent almost half of her life in foreign countries in exile, yet she never forgot her faith or beliefs. She was greatly influenced by the beliefs and principles of her faith. Before we set out to know more about the Zoroastrian religion, let us find a little about the glorious past of the Parsis settled in India.

In the sixth century B.C., a great Persian empire had been established in Persepolis; it ruled over twenty continents and twenty countries over a long period of time. The Zoroastrianism was their royal faith. Millions of its followers spread right from Rome to Indus River. Passing through the cycles of rise and fall over centuries, the followers of this faith fled from Persia (now Iran) when they were targeted by the Muslim invaders. The first group of refugees arrived on the Diu island of Gujarat in between the eight and the tenth century. Those days, the local ruler of that place was Jadav Rana.

Conditions of Jadav Rana

Jadav Rana did not say a word himself, but he sent a bowl of milk to Dastur Naryosang, the Parsis' priest. It meant that they were undesirable in his country; however, the priest was witty and wise; he too replied symbolically; he returned the bowl of milk now mixed with some sugar. It signified that the Parsis would live in complete harmony with the local people, much like sugar dissolve in milk.

At this, Jadav Rana placed certain conditions laid before them:

- They will explain the meaning of their faith to the religious head here.
- They will adopt Gujarati as their mother tongue.
- The Parsi women will wear sarees.
- They will have to deposit all their arms.
- They will conduct their marriage ceremonies after sunset.
- They will take out their processions only after sunset.

The priest accepted terms. They were now sanctioned to live abiding by their faith and customs, and to bring up their children as per their assumptions. They also got some land for farming.

This was how the Parsi people mixed themselves in the local environment. Their holy text was translated into Sanskrit. The book *Kissa-e-Sanjan* (The Tales of Sanjan) gives a number of historical details about them. These people lived in Sanjan, from where they had to flee in the fifteenth century due to the Muslim invasion. They carried their holy fire, called *Naksahi* with them, and established their fire temple. Mutual discord caused by the priests, this holy fire was shifted to Udavada. That place remains an important place of pilgrimage for the Parsis.

Parsis' Mercantile Development

In the sixteenth century A.D., Surat became an important trade centre. The Parsis too came and settled here, because they carried out trade with the British. Towards the onset of the nineteenth century, they were migrated to Bombay, because famine had made the financial conditions of Gujarat quite mirthless, while Bombay was progressing rapidly on the industrial front.

In the beginning, farming was their chief occupation, but soon, due to their accute vision, they adopted profession like, carpentry, ship-building and brokering etc. They started to visit neighbouring countries in connection with trade. It is said that the religious principles of the Parsis were also translated in the royal court of Akbar.

Parsi Community and Education

The Parsi community had realized the actual importance of education much earlier. By 1870, more than one hundred Parsi girls had completed primary and secondary education. The Parsis did not take time to go for western education in the fields of medicine, law and engineering. They occupied important political posts also. It would be needless to state that they gave a profound contribution in the progress and development of the contemporary society.

In 1892, Dada Bhai Naoroji was nominated to the

British House of Commons; he was the first Indian to have received this honour.

Parsi Community and Country's Progress

The Parsi community has contributed significantly in every area for the development of India. The Parsis possessed financial resources as well as technology of cotton cloth industry; it was due to them that this industry was established in the country. Jamshedji Tata founded the hydroelectric project, and laid the foundation for the iron and steel industry in Jamshedpur. He had also established the first scientific institution in the country.

Although Parsis adopted the policy to largely remain neutral in India's freedom struggle, but there had have been a number of Parsi men and women who had given excellent contribution for it, such as Dada Bhai Naoroji, Ferozeshah Mehta, Dinshaw Bachha and Madam Cama, etc. are leading personalities.

Other leading luminaries of this community, who have shone in different fields, comprise Sam Manekshaw, Homi Jahangir J. Bhabha, Suni Taraporewala, Jamshedji Tata, Wadia, Godrej and Nani F. Palkiwala etc.

In one of his speeches, Dada Bhai Naoroji had said: "Whatever I might be: Hindu, Muslim, Parsi, Christian or the follower of any other faith, I remain an Indian first and foremost."

If we don't include the names of the true nationalists like Barjorji Framji Bharucha and Feroze Gandhi, it would be injustice. Speaking about Feroze

Gandhi, Mahatma Gandhi had said: "If I can get seven youths like Feroze to work with me, I have no doubt that I can get Swaraj within seven days."

Perin Captain, granddaughter of Dada Bhai Naoroji, worked as a dedicated worker and supporter of Gandhiji. The Parsi women did not lag behind in motivating the Indian women to join the Indian freedom struggle.

Religious belief of Madam Cama

Zoroastrian religion and Madam Cama were lifelong friend. She had to live a life under very different circumstances, which might have helped her to adapt with the western culture; till the end, she continued to follow the traditions and customs of her faith honestly.

Undoubtedly, she possessed modern views, yet she never cast away wearing Sudraha and Kusti, the symbols of her faith.

Sudraha is a white cotton cloth, worn inside, with a V-shape neck. It has a small pocket just under the neck, which is called 'pocket of good deeds'. It reminds the wearer that our good deeds won't measure more than one square inch if compared with God's goodness. Man ought to fill this pocket with his good deeds.

Kusti is a sacred thread, which is a symbol of religious languages. This is made from seventy-two woolen strands; a special prayer is conducted while weaving it. This thread is worn over Sudraha. It is wrapped round the waist thrice with knots to the front and back. All Zoroastrian children are taught a small prayer in their childhood, called Ahunvar or *Athaovar*.

Several of her friends have mentioned in their memoirs that Madam Cama kept repeating the prayer of *Ahunvar* all the time. She always kept a copy of *Zed Avesta*, their holy text, with her. In all her photographs, she can be seen wearing the traditional saree, one end of which covers her head. This was the pure Indian traditional form of that aggressive revolutionary.

□

2

Contact with the Motherland

Bhikaji Cama was born on 24 September, 1861 in a wealthy Parsi family of Bombay. Her father was Sorabji Framji Patel and mother, Jijabai. Sorabji was a well-known trader of Bombay. The women of Parsi community were considered quite modern even in those times. They were quite conscious when it came to women empowerment, rights and education.

Bhikaji did her primary and secondary education from Alexandra Girls Education Institution; it was considered the best women school in the country then. She was called Munni affectionately at home. The nature of Madam Cama from the begining was significantly different amongst her nine brothers and sisters. She had learnt a number of languages in her childhood itself.

Environment in the Parsi Community

The contemporary Parsis were considered as the supporters of the English. The family of Bhikaji had a clear impression of wealth and elitist class.

The prosperous family was permeated with a clear impression of the western culture and civilization. All ostentatious and magnificent goods were procured from abroad. The houses were often decorated with the pictures of English emperors. Governesses were employed for education and taking good care of their children.

The Parsis took no time to adopt English and other European languages promptly and with interest. They also adopted the games played by the English.

It may be appropriate to say here that they could lead their life at par with the English. The women in their families wore sarees in the traditional Parsi style, but they were not prohibited from mixing up with men during public and social functions. Thus, the Parsi women were not restrained within the four walls and limited to the Kitchen of the house. They were completely aware of the prevailing political and economic conditions of the country.

The young Bhikaji too grew up in such a free and prosperous environment. She got opportunities to mix up with the high class society as well as to discuss on different current topics. Maybe due to this, she possessed rebellious feelings against the British oppression, despite she was brought up under the care of the English.

Building of Personality

Bhikaji was not influenced by the English environment. Undoubtedly, she wore fashionable dresses and met the foreign community freely. It was due to her modern and vigorous nature that she had interest in cricket too. During those times, cricket was a field exclusively meant for men.

Bhikaji spent first thirty years of her life among such people who wanted the country to be brought forward in terms of modernity; however, they were little concerned about the freedom of the country. Bhikaji was not unaware of the events taking place outside the four walls of the house. Soon, she dreamt of freeing India from the English oppression and exploitation.

Wedding

Bhikaji's marriage was fixed in a wealthy and respectable family of Bombay. Her would be father-in-law was Khujshedji Rustam Cama, the well-known professor of Oriental studies. She had special faith in her father-in-law, and bowed in respect of his wisdom and knowledge.

Her fiancé's name was Rustam Cama. He was a well-educated, wealthy and handsome young man, who belonged to the well-known family. At least her friends considered that it was fortunate for Bhikaji to get such a fine young man as her husband. Rustamji was an attorney by profession. Any girl could have considered herself lucky to be his wife, since in those days, the scope of women was generally restricted to wedding, offspring and household.

Madam Bhikaji was married on 3 August, 1885. No doubt, it was the most important event of her life; however, the first session of the Indian National Congress was no less significant for her. The newly-wed Cama seemed to have chosen two contradictory and opposite paths for herself simultaneously. One path led her towards her household duties at her husband's house, while the other path was a thorny one, where she was not likely to get anything but only, loneliness, suffering and disrespect.

Bhikaji observed the Congress working, and was convinced that in the years to come, the Congress was bound to contribute towards India's freedom, and at the same time, it would work for women emancipation too.

Resolve for Patriotism

Madam Cama's husband, Rustamji had little interest in public life. He considered the British rulers as compassionate and possessed quite illiberal views. Due to this, differences arose between him and his wife right from the beginning, and then this mental gap started to widen with time.

Madam Cama thought that she had been married to an ideal young man, in spite of that she had entered into an alliance with the countrymen having social and political viewpoints. The country was calling her; how long could she unheard the call from her country and her heart.

If she wished, she could have lived a fine and comfortable life with her husband, could have worn the costliest dresses and jewellery, could have enjoyed all the luxuries of life; but she had taken the vow of serving the nation. An individual, who has vowed to do something for the country, feels nothing else more pleasant than this.

Differences with Husband

Rustamji was one of those people who were supporters of British rule in India. He believed that it was to be so in the interest of the country. However, in the beginning, he had assisted his wife in undertaking social reforms. He had helped in editing a journal on social reforms published by Madam Cama. Even so everything was fine, but he did not like his wife should have access to social service on the roads and hutment for the poor people.

In 1896, an epidemic of plague broke out in Bombay. Madam Cama renounced the comfort of her wealthy family, and involved herself completely in serving the suffering people. Bhikaji served wearing a white apron, she was not less looked like Florence Nightingale in this dress.

The family members of Rustamji thought that it was a childish act of their daughter-in-law to do all this, and she would leave doing all this with passage of time, but Bhikaji knew that she was in her proper senses. She found her in-laws supporting the English decorum and rule, meanwhile she was engaged in anti-British activities. Her husband now irritated with her wife's social and political life.

Despite his unhappiness, Cama continued to work for the people suffering from plague. How courageous she was, can be ascertained from the fact that she risked her life to serve the people, even though no vaccine to check the spread of plague had been discovered upto that time.

This matter was no less than a great disrespect for her own family and her in-laws'; they did not want that she should visit public hospitals and poor settlements for serving the poor.

Madam Cama who had to attend the parties of the elitist people, and had to become a status symbol she was the pride of Rustamji's family, seeing this look of her they lost their temper, which resulted into a graver animosity between Madam Cama and her husband daily.

Social Service to Revolution

Madam Cama entered public life through social service. She could no longer bear the English atrocities in the name of controlling plague. In the beginning, she took part in political activities through the Congress, and finally became a part of the extremist and revolutionary activities.

In 1901, Bhikaji fell ill and the doctors advised her to go abroad for treatment.

□

3

The Mother of Revolution is Born

Though Madam Cama the revolutionary had been born much earlier, but in true sense of the term, the 'mother of revolution' was born only after she went to London. It was like a new birth for her. The beloved daughter of a prosperous Parsi family, who was the daughter-in-law of a well-educated and wealthy family, was now about to enter a new world which was eclipsed by the specter of uncertainties, and misery; pervaded by penury and scarcity; enveloped by thick darkness of setbacks and humiliation. However, the only source of light among all these was the indomitable desire to get the country freed. This feeling of independence of each obstacles remain retort.

When the illness, that inflicted Cama, could not be diagnosed in India, the doctors advised to send her to England. The well-wishers as well as family members wished that she should go abroad for recovery. Possibly her husband too wanted this because he hoped that she would also be cured of her ghost of patriotism; however, he little realized that the true children of Mother India never waver from their vow. It was how Madam Cama had been forced to go out of India.

Madam Cama left for England in 1901. When her ship set the sail, she looked at the motherland with moist eyes. At this hour, she little knew that she would have to be stay away from her motherland for as long as thirty-five years.

Sojourn in London

Madam Cama recovered after a successful surgery and medical treatment; now she stayed as a paying guest with a respectable family in the Holborn area. That was the beginning of her political and revolutionary life. She now started actively campaigning against the British rule in India. Before settling in London, she also stayed one year each in Germany, Scotland and France. This gave her opportunity to expand her network in the political spectrum, and fundamental changes in her political ideology and doctrine.

Dada Bhai Naoroji, a senior leader, was also there those days. Madam Cama started to work as his private secretary. With him, she shared the work of the Indian National Congress. It was through Naoroji that she got an opportunity to come into contact with many people working in politics. Different languages gave a new dimension to her thinking. Now the question of 'Personal freedom' had become all the more manifest.

Meeting with Revolutionaries

Madam Cama was profoundly influenced by the views of Mazzini, the great Italian revolutionary leader. Those days, the important Indians like Shyamji Krishna Varma, Sardar Singh Revabhai Rana and Sarojini Naidu were staying in London. London was also a popular place of refuge for revolutionaries belonging to other countries.

It was H.M. Hyndman who first opposed the policies adopted by the Congress leaders. Madam Cama, Shyamji Krishna Varma and S.S. Rana too were dissatisfied with the British Committee of the Indian National Congress. Hyndman suggested to spread awareness on this count through newspapers. He had knowledge of the importance of press and media for communicating ideas.

Madam Cama started to deliver speeches openly in Hyde Park in which she supported India's independence. Such effort on the part of a woman, especially one who belonged to India, was a matter of pleasant surprise for people. Its impact might have been slow, but her efforts finally bore fruit. The Indian immigrants in London started to support her ideology that India should be given freedom.

Meanwhile, India was facing a flood of extremist movements. A number of violent incidents had taken place after the breakout of plague. Along with this the oppression of the government also started with high speed. Writers and poets protested against this through their pens.

A Novel Course

Shyamji Krishna Varma was conducting the Indian revolution from London. He started publishing an English monthly magazine, named *The Indian Sociologist* from 1905. Its philosophical page was used for propaganda of revolution. He stated in it:

"Protest against atrocity is not only proper but also compulsory. Keeping the political relations between England and India in view, an Indian interpreter is needed in England on behalf of India, who could tell the government here how the Indians were reeling under the shackles of the British rule."

Dada Bhai Naoroji had introduced Madam Cama with Sardar Singh Rana, who on those days was a student of the Inner Temple of Inns of Court. It was through him that she met Shyamji Krishna Varma. After she learned the fine points of politics from Dada Bhai Naoroji, she joined these revolutionaries to choose a path which made her an extreme nationalist.

Madam Cama started to write for *The Indian Sociologist* regularly. The chief objective of this paper was to demand complete home rule in India.

On the other hand, the annual sessions of the Congress kept expanding the scope of their demands. Undoubtedly, these demands and resolutions were helpful in building a popular opinion; however, many persons came to the forefront who did not wish to wait patiently. These were the people who did not shy away from attacking the British rule openly.

A number of anti-British centres had come into existence in Europe and America too. It was through these centres that extremist and inciting revolutionary literature was propagated. These revolutionaries were fully supported by revolutionaries from Ireland, Egypt and Russia.

Shyamji Krishna Varma, who believed in strikes and non-cooperative methods, too wrote in the newspaper: "Whatever the reason, the people of India have no more faith in the constitutional movement. It appears that it is becoming incumbent to run a secret movement in India. We will have to adopt the Russian means vigorously in order to bring the British round to our viewpoint."

That period was a time of great upheaval in the Indian history. Madam Cama started to work for freedom actively in cooperation with revolutionary associates. Madam Cama possessed belief in constitutional methods of protest, but now the circumstances transformed her into an aggressive nationalist; and she adopted this path willingly, because in her view, any means was justifiable for attaining freedom, howsoever dangerous or tumultuous it might be.

□

4

The House of Terror

'The House of Terror', 'The House of Mystery', 'The Beehive', 'The Devil and His Dirty Dozen' and 'Lair'! Yes, of course, these were the nomenclatures that were given to the India House in London by the British Intelligence department. This three-storey building, covered with dense bushes, wild vines and low boundaries, was quite important in the life of Madam Cama. She did not live here, but all her activities were centred in the India House.

This was the centre of activities of her comrade revolutionaries, who delivered motivating speeches, undertook different types of activities, wrote articles and conducted meetings. This place had, in fact, been founded by Shyamji Krishna Varma. On a cursory look it was a place where 25-30 people could stay, where Indian food was available, where Indian students studying abroad lived; but it was in fact a revolutionary centre of young Indians who were opposing the British rule in India.

This building also had a lecture room, a library and a recreation room. Students could avail its facilities by paying only Rs. 16 a week. Later, this place grew to be such a popular centre of Indian revolutionary movement by the name of which even the Intelligence Bureau was scared.

Shyamji Krishna Varma, founder of India House and a revolutionary politician, was of the view that India's freedom is only dependent on the Indians. He opined that the foreign rule would not sustain any longer and will be wiped out completely once the Indians stop serving their British masters.

Inauguration Ceremony

The India House was inaugurated on 1 July, 1905. This ceremony was attended by the journalists of all prominent newspapers, representatives of all political parties of England, Mr. Hyndman, Mr. Harry Quelch Madam Charlotte Despard, Mr. Swinney, Madam Cama, Dada Bhai Naoroji, Lala Lajpat Rai, Hansraj, Dost Mohammad and a number of other Indian students.

In his address, Shyamji expressed gratitude to Dada Bhai Naoroji, who had chosen to attend the ceremony despite his differences on political ideology. Hyndman delivered a historical speech on this occasion. He said: "As things stands, loyalty to Great Britain simply means betrayal against India. I have met a number of Indians, and most of them have displayed their devotion and loyalty towards the British rule; this is in fact disgusting; they are either ignorant, or they lack honesty, though I am happy that new spirit and vitality are coming into existence. The men and women belonging to different races, who have gathered here this evening, do not hold the same ideology, but they all have a common goal, that is the independence of India."

"It is pointless to have high hopes from England. Only resolute revolutionaries and those who are bent upon sacrificing themselves for the national cause, can find a way for India's freedom."

"The founding of the India House is a step towards India's freedom and progress; and maybe, some of the men and women gathered here could become witness to the remarkable success of this enterprise."

Madam Cama and India House

Madam Cama's heart got stirred to hear these words. There was no doubt that she was assisting in every step that was being taken up for India's freedom.

Although, she was no more a youth, but she cared little for her health and kept herself busy in her political life. Weekly meetings were held in the India House. It was here that she formulated plans to carry forward the movement in conjunction with the revolutionaries like S.S. Rana, Hardayal, Senapati Bapat, Virendranath Chattopadhyay, Parmanand, M.P.T. Acharya and Veer Savarkar.

However, Gandhiji considered the people of the India House as a 'violent team', yet he also appreciated them for their intellectual prowess, truthfulness and spirit of self-sacrifice.

At that time, this place was the source of inspiration for a number of young Indians staying abroad. The India House was initiating Indians into the spirit of revolution. The young men, who had gone there to get good education and employment, even they forgot their selfish interests here and vowed to engage themselves in the service of the nation.

When Veer Savarkar became the leader of the India House, he formed a committee called Abhinav Bharat. It conducted meetings on a regular basis. It celebrated birthdays of revolutionaries and Indian festivals, as well as conducted condolence assemblies, and the like. It may not be exaggerated to say that every positive and negative event found due expression there.

Madam Cama took part in all these activities enthusiastically. She had got a means by which she could concretize her abstract ideologies. Whenever revolutionaries sat together, such aggressive and vigorous views came to the fore which could shake the foundation of the English rule in India.

Every possible step was taken in order to inculcate ardent spirit and desire for freedom in the countrymen. In no time, the place replaced the theoretical aggression of Shyamji Krishna Varma with aggressive and treasonous activities.

In this connection, Veer Savarkar wrote a book titled *the First War of Indian Independence.* The British government too came to know about it. The book had been seized even before it could be published.

Madam Cama and Veer Savarkar became aware that they would have to propagate their ideas at the international level, so that the countries of the world could know about the actual prevailing conditions in India.

They wrote fiery articles and speeches in order to draw the favour of sympathetic Englishmen and international leaders towards India's politics. These articles were translated into French, Italian, German, Portuguese and Russian languages for distribution to the target audience. Madam Cama translated Savarkar's book into French. It was the same book which had become very important for the revolutionaries; they considered it as their *Geeta*, the source of inspiration. In the beginning of each meeting and conference in the India House, the revolutionaries sang *Vande Mataram*. Before they went to bed, they recited a collective prayer, which said:

Ek devata, ek desh, ek bhasha;
Ek jati, ek jeev, ek aasha.
(One God, one country, one language;
One race, one being, one hope.)

Anti-British Front

Veer Savarkar wanted that a joint anti-British front should be constituted so that all hands can join together for the revolt. As this revolt needed weapons, he took upon himself the responsibility for writing and printing work as well as undertook responsibility for stimulating and explosive propaganda through literature.

In London there was no place where the revolutionaries could take training of weapons. There were some rifle shooting clubs, but Indians were kept out of them. The revolutionaries of the India House undertook target practice at a desolate place. Not only this, some people also worked on the technique of bomb-making. They wanted to send this technique to India in a book form, so that other revolutionary can also take advantage by it.

Golden Jubilee Celebration of First War of Independence

The India House celebrated the golden jubilee of the First War of Independence. Its convener was Shyamji Krishna Varma. He proposed for the chairman of the celebration as:

"For this glorious celebration, I propose the name of the great revolutionary Sardar Singh Rana as the chairman. I hope that you all will approve it."

All of them supported the resolution unanimously. After this, the portraits of Nana Saheb Peshwa, Tatya Tope and Maharani Lakshmi Bai were unveiled.

Madam Cama could not attend this function. S.S. Rana read out her message, an extract of which is as follows:

"Today is a day of great inspiration and pride for all Indians. Today, we are celebrating the Golden Jubilee of the Mahayagna, the First War of Independence of our country. We bow before all those known and unknown eternal souls who offered their lives for the country's freedom. May those brave souls strengthen, energize and motivate us to follow their glorious paths"

In this function, S.S. Rana donated his income for the following month to the Martyr Fund. Despite British opposition, Madam Cama got Savarkar's book published secretly and sent one of its copies to Maxim Gorky in Russia too.

In India, Subhash Chandra Bose released the English edition of this book, while Bhagat Singh released its Hindi edition. This was that the courage of Madam Cama bore fruit by which different types of revolutionary literature could be made available at different places.

Detectives under Watch

The India House was the place where different types of impassioned and fiery literature were made available by Madam Cama and Savarkar. When the government banned their literature, they found a novel way to send it across to Pondicherry (now Puducherry) in India. The revolutionaries used to write booklets in thousands, which were printed without any name and address, and then they were sent to hundreds of different addresses.

The revolutionary youths had found their perfect and concrete goal under the leadership of Madam Cama. She often said to them:

"Independent India will be a republic, Hindi will be its national language and Devnagri its national script." All revolutionaries took a pledge to do something and die for the country.

Meanwhile, in the ears of British detectives had also become aware of these activities. They were on the lookout, they kept the place under watch, but they failed to find any clue. Finally, they placed an informer named Kirtikar in the India House.

This youth said that he was studying dentistry. The greatest problem that the detectives faced was that the Indian revolutionaries often used to speak in different Indian languages in order to deceive the detectives. This made it quite impossible for them to know what was going on there.

When Kirtikar started to live in India House and started to leak out the activities being conducted there, but the revolutionaries had soon become suspicious of him. One day, a revolutionary entered his class to find more about him. There he came to know that he had never attended the dentistry class. It simply meant that he was not an Indian student.

The same night, the revolutionaries entered his room to search it thoroughly. They found all the records that he had sent to the Intelligence Bureau. When threatened, this man revealed everything and admitted his guilt.

In order not to let the Intelligence Bureau know about this revelation, he was asked to continue to send the similar reports, these reports were now edited and censored by Vinayak Damodar Savarkar. Thus, only that information which the revolutionaries wished the government detectives to know was made available.

□

5

Imprisonment of Lala Lajpat Rai

When the golden jubilee of the 1857 revolt was being celebrated in the India House, back in India, the same day the British government arrested Sardar Ajit Singh and Lala Lajpat Rai. They both were taken to an undisclosed place. The entire country was grief-stricken at this development. This news did not take much time to reach the India House too. Though the revolutionaries there, like Madam Cama and Shyamji, were not able to do anything in this, yet they protested against this atrocious step in *The Indian Sociologist*.

Shyamji wrote: "Arrest of Lala Lajpat Rai is an occurrence which can be called a presage of the decline of the British rule in India. The highest ideals of renunciation and diligence that Lala Lajpat Rai has placed before the countrymen, will continue to inspire them and will assure them of the truth that all the steps that the world has taken towards progress, have only traversed from one set of gallows to the next, and from one disaster to the next."

An Appeal

In her emotional words, Madam Cama said to her countrymen:

"Brothers and sisters,

"I rose one morning to regretfully know that our comrade and true patriot, Lala Lajpat Rai has been arrested from his house.

"Men and women of India, you all should step ahead to protest against this cruel repression. Decide that you will not tolerate this bondage anymore, even to the peril of your lives.

"What is the use to appreciate ancient glory of India, Persia and Arabia if you continue to live a life of slavery? Brave Rajputs, Sikhs, Pathans, Gurkhas, patriot Marathas, Bengalis, perseverant Parsis, courageous Muslims, humble Jains, Oh! enduring offspring of great and powerful races - Hindus, why are you not abiding by your high traditions? What is cause which forces you to remain under bondage? Break away these bonds. Establish self-rule and equality.

"Brothers and sisters, fight for human rights and tell the West that the East can teach them many a thing. Teach a hard lesson to the English who had been delineated by William Wordsworth, the grandson of the famous poet Wordsworth, as 'the devils in white dresses'.

"I wish if I could smash the prison doors and bring out Lala Lajpat Rai, we could not leave such a patriot to breathe in the polluted air of the jail.

"Our strength lies in unity. Come, let us all be united. If all of us follow the path that of Lala Lajpat Rai, if we speak the same voice he spoke, this English government will have to build a very large number of jails and forts to imprison all of us. Our population stands at about fifty crores. If we all learn to be Lala Lajpat Rai, it would not take much time to be united. Come, let us take up his goal as our own, and let his suffering be our own grief.

"Indian youths! you are the bridge to link the past and the future. Though we cannot set our feet on our country, yet we can at least remember our country to our last breath. Come, follow this unshakable principle. Let us not forget that freedom has to be conquered, it is not given in inheritance.

"We must not forget these brave people during this freedom struggle who have sacrificed themselves on the altar of the motherland.

"Friends, awaken your self-respect. Don't work for the oppressive rulers. Sever your relations with them. Resign from their jobs, and then you will see that it would take no time to bring this autocratic regime to paralyze. I wish I could come to you to tell all this myself, but my failing health does not allow me to do so.

May God raise the entire India inspired by *Vande Mataram*." (*Paris, The Indian Sociologist, June 1907*)

Madam Cama had appealed to follow the strategies of non-cooperation and voluntary offer for arrest years before they came into existence.

This is a well-known fact that how effective these strategies proved to be in the times to come. Not only leaders, but millions of Indians adopted these mantras from the core of their hearts and succeeded in getting long-awaited freedom.

□

6

Hoist the Flag High

The national flag is a symbol of honour. Every citizen of the country respects the national flag, and is also ready to sacrifice his life for its sake. He follows its dignity always.

Today you can find the national flag hoisted on government and semi-government buildings gloriously; but there was a time when it was a legal offence to hoist this symbol of independent expression. During the twentieth century when our country was struggling to get free from the British rule, the freedom fighters needed a symbol in the form of a flag; they needed a flag under which all Indians could express their views proudly. The history of the national flag is quite interesting.

The Tricolour that we see today, has taken its present form through a number of fantasies, and ideas in different forms. In this context, we shall first discuss the flag as imagined by Sister Nivedita.

Flag of Sister Nivedita

For quite some time, Nivedita was thinking of a national flag. She wrote to one of her friends: "We have decided upon the shape of the Indian national flag, and it is *Vajra*. I have made the first design. Unfortunately, keeping the Chinese battle colours in view, I made a black *Vajra* (lightning, an ancient weapon) on red background; however, the Indians are not likely to accept it, so I made another pattern, which is a yellow pattern on a saffron background."

Her idea about the national flag was as follows:

"A national flag can be a boon, as well as a bane. It is a symbol of respect and glory, while it also functions as a basis for hollow announcements at times. under its base there may also be brutal murders, while people can sacrifice their blood for its protection. It is pious like the land for *Yajna* or sacrifice, this symbol will continue to be eternal. It has a great impact on the people who possess faith on it."

She wanted to use *Vajra* on the flag as the symbol of Indian honour, because according to the ancient traditions, *Vajra* has been taken as the symbol of respect, purity, wisdom, virtue and energy. The flag by Sister Nivedita was appreciated by well-known people and approved it for use.

Use of Three Colours for First Time

In 1906, after the partition of Bengal, people rose in protest, processions were taken out. In these processions, Shachindra Kumar Bose used a three-colour flag. This flag had a stripe of saffron colour at the top, yellow in the middle and green at the bottom. On the saffron stripe were made eight half-bloomed lotus flowers. The green colour stripe had a sun and a moon, while in the yellow stripe in the middle was written the word *Vandemataram*.

Berlin Committee Flag

Today we shall talk about a flag which was unfurled proudly at an international stage for the first time in front of hundreds of foreigners. This flag is also known as Berlin Committee Flag, because it was adopted by the Indian revolutionaries in Berlin Committee.

Memorable Moments of Life

On 22 August, 1907, the International Socialist convention was about to be held at Stuttgart in Germany. In the Congress sessions held before this, India was represented by Dada Bhai Naoroji. Everybody wished that this time the people of the extremist faction should represent India. This congress was attended by Madam Cama, Virendranath Chattopadhyay and Sardar Singh Rana.

When people saw Madam Cama, adorned in a Parsi saree with a full-sleeved blouse, sitting with a glorious face, people started to whisper in low voices. Her head was covered with an end of her saree, which displayed her courtesy, but when the same courteous and well-cultured Indian woman rose to speak in a fluent style, it appeared as if the entire assembly had been put on fire. When the Union Jack was about to be hoisted as mark of the national flag of India, she opposed it and took out a small Tricolour from her bag and waved it in her hands. With this, she said:

"Dignitaries, this is the flag of India's freedom. Look, this has taken birth. The great martyrs of India have shed their blood to approve of it. Gentlemen, I entreat that you all must salute this Indian flag by standing at your places. Taking this Tricolour as witness, I appeal to the freedom-lovers all over the world that they should assist in freeing one-fifth of the world's population."

It was Madam Cama who hoisted the national flag on the foreign soil for the first time to draw the world's attention towards the country's problems. Everybody stood up on their feet, expressed their deference for it and clapped in its honour. When all of them took back their seats, Madam Cama thanked them and said: "You all freedom-loving gentlemen have respected a country's flag that wishes for freedom; I thank all of you on behalf of all of my countrymen."

Demand for Complete Freedom

In political history of India, the demand for sovereign freedom was first put forward by none else than Madam Cama. She moved the resolution as: "The government of any completely social state government is not oppressive, persistence of the

British rule in India is very harmful and dangerous; therefore, you all should unite to…"

It was for the first time at the international level that the British were asked in clear terms to quit India. The British delegation opposed the resolution. No one objected to the hoisting of the flag by Madam Cama or her speech, but a technical basis was discovered to stop voting on the resolution.

It was claimed that the resolution had not been sent to the international office before moving it in the Congress, therefore, it could not be considered. Though most of the leaders were sympathetic in favour of the resolution, yet this technicality could not be overcome. Hyndman himself supported the demand raised by Madam Cama.

The resolution could not be passed, but the Indian delegation moved the resolution under the aegis of the Tricolour, and thus could the real face of the British was exposed; can it be called any trivial achievement?

Participation in Socialist Congress

A Socialist Congress convention was held at Stockholm in which the Indians who wished to participate in it were told that—"India could not take part in it since there was no socialist party in the country..." At this, the desirous people took part in the Congress convention in their personal capacity.

Due to her contacts with prominent socialists of Europe, Madam Cama could pose as a representative. She knew that the delegation from Russia was taking part in it, so she said:

"Our country is poor; therefore, it could not send its delegation, but I am hopeful that a day would come when they all will rise and follow the Russian comrades in their footsteps. We especially offer our good wishes to those who are struggling for their freedom."

First National Flag of India

The most popular picture of Bhikaji Rustam Cama is the one in which see her standing up holding Tricolour in her hands. In fact, this flag has become the chief cause of her popularity. The flag can be called the symbol of the aspirations and ambitions of any country.

Madam Cama and Savarkar had together prepared the pattern of this flag. Some biographers have gone to the extent of saying that Madam Cama had torn an edge of her saree to make the flag and unfurled it; however, it remains pure imagination. A lot of thought process was involved in its making.

This flag had three broad horizontal stripes. On the top of it, green colour denoted greenery of India, it is also considered the sacred colour by the Muslims. In the middle was the saffron stripe, which is considered sacred in Hinduism. The third stripe was red, which is considered a symbol of bravery as Indian warriors sacrificed their blood for their motherland.

In the top stripe of green colour were embossed eight lotus flowers; at that time, India was divided into eight provinces, and eight lotus flowers could also indicate the Yoga system of India. The middle stripe of saffron colour had the sun and the moon embossed on it. These could indicate unity between Hindus and Muslims. The symbols of different people living in India had found a place in the flag.

The words that Madam Cama uttered in the Socialist conference resonated in the air for a long time to come, so did the discussion about her hoisting the national flag. A German newspaper wrote thus:

"The Congress touched its zenith at the moment when Madam Cama, wearing a silver silk saree, ascended the stage. She appealed for help for the suffering countrymen who were reeling under the British atrocities; and in the end, she waved the silken Tricolour as a mark of the flag of the suffering people. It resulted into a continuous clapping sound for a long time...."

Memoirs of Kamala Devi

Several years later, a elite and talented lady of India, Kamala Devi Chattopadhyay got an opportunity to meet Madam Cama. Recalling her anecdote, she said:

"I met another well-known personality in Europe, Madam Cama, though I was aware that a young revolutionary of Bombay lived in Paris, but it was the first opportunity to meet her.

"Despite her age, she had maintained faith and devotion in country's independence. I was greatly pleased to meet her. She possessed a delicate personality. When we sat and talked, I told her how we had made a national flag in the women congress in Berlin. Listening to this, she held my hand and then hugged me. It appeared as if this mother of revolution had blessed me solemnly."

Whereabouts of the Historical Flag

The flag hoisted in Calcutta in 1906 and the flag that Madam Cama hoisted in the Congress in 1907, these are quite amazingly similar in pattern. Maybe, the Indian revolutionaries who made its pattern might have kept in mind the previous flag.

The flag that accompanied along with Madam Cama was adopted by all the revolutionaries wholeheartedly. In her speeches, she often said:

"This is the same flag for which Khudiram and Prafulla Chaki sacrificed their lives."

Indulal Yajnik, the socialist leader of Gujarat, brought it to India by hiding secretly along with other revolutionary records. On his arrival here, he kept all this material at some secret place.

He was arrested in 1939. Those days, he was in Yarvada Jail. He called G.V. Ketkar in the jail and handed him over a slip of paper.

It was on the basis of this piece of paper that Ketkar could find out the flag and secret documents of the revolutionaries. The flag was mounted in a magnificent frame and taken out in a splendid procession.

Today, this flag is hung in the library chamber of the office of the *Kesari* and *Maratha* in Pune. Every visitor bows in front of it with all respect and dedication, and recalls its historical importance which fills him with pride.

□

7

American Tour

A few weeks after she hoisted the flag at the International Socialist Congress, Madam Cama had planned for her tour to America so that the people there could be apprised of the pitiable condition prevailing in India, and find their support. She arrived there in October 1907, as soon as she reached there, she started her movement. Though she was not in favour of her propaganda, but it was necessary for her to take to stage in order to place her point before the people; and in this process, she grew to be quite popular amongst the Americans. The American press called her Indian Zone of Arch.

During this, an interesting incident took place. The American press was quite enthusiastic about the arrival of an Indian woman. However, that the Indians prior to her arrival had to face great many obstacles there. The American society, environment and mentality remained unfavourable to them, because the Americans had nothing to do with the Indian political problems. They neither knew of these, nor did they possess any sympathetic attitude for the Indians. Swami Vivekananda had tried to change this attitude to a greater extent and succeeded too. But Madam Cama was welcomed here nicely.

Yet she had not even reached America, a large picture of hers was published in the media. In that picture, an Indian woman had been shown wearing a large shawl over her head staring at the onlookers with burning eyes. All this was quite amazing as well as humorous for Madam Cama. Later, on remembering this she often laughed at this imaginary picture of hers. She had told her comrades about this picture too.

Speeches and Meetings

As soon as she arrived in America, she got busy in her programmes of speeches and meetings. She had gone there with a clear and definite goal; so there was no doubt in her mind of any kind regarding her mission.

In an interview given to *The Sun*, she said:

"We are slaves. The sole purpose of my arrival here is to expose the oppressions and atrocities being unleashed by the British rule in India, so that I may get your country's support for achieving freedom for our people.

"England is taking away all the wealth of our country. Annually, it takes our wealth worth as much as three and a half crore pounds out of our country. As a consequence, thousands of our people perish, and those who survive, they survive only on the donations given by America. We wish that our countrymen too get education in a western manner. We have our own culture, but country needs funds to get independence."

Then she said: "We who are outraged no one have concern for them. I am confident that I will be able to return to India one day. Recently, two well-cultured and civilized individuals have been arrested and exiled; their only crime was that they were telling about the actual situation of the country; these days, they are in Burma."

Thus, wherever Madam Cama went, wherever she spoke, there, before an audience, clear picture emerged about atrocities in India. In September 1907, one month before Madam Cama arrived in America, the Indo-American National Association had been established. In November 1907, this association had been renamed. The key objectives of this association comprised giving cooperation to Indian students in America, bridging the gap between India and America and drawing the American citizens' sympathy towards Indians.

During her sojourn in America, Madam Cama stayed with S.L. Joshi, secretary of the Pan-Aryan association. In her speeches, she enunciated the purpose of her visit to America and said in clear terms that what India wanted was home rule.

Glorious Past of India

Like other nationalists, Madam Cama too believed in ancient glorious culture and civilization of India. Mentioning about the spiritual contribution of Swami Vivekananda, she said:

"The people of India have the wealth of culture. Even the poorest farmer in the village knows about the spiritual truths contained in the *Ramayana* and *Mahabharata*. We are of the opinion that it would be improper to impose Christianity on such simple and spiritual people by the force of gun."

Once a British journalist asked her how the end of British rule could be possible. At this, she said:

"It is possible through the civil disobedience. Our native are voters of peace, and they possess no arms. We cannot fight even if we wish to. What is enough to do is to refuse to work for them. In only five days a massive revolution will occur in which not a drop of blood will be shed."

Servant of a Slave Country

The people of America considered Madam Cama as the one who talked of violence, revolution and blood-shedding; but when she arrived there, they came to know that she possessed a unique image; she referred to the ancient philosophy and civilization of India. With her charm, Madam Cama had fascinated them all.

When a journalist from *The Sun* interviewed her, Madam Cama pleaded with her as follows:

"I plead with you not to publish in newspapers that I am a princess of some place. I may not be introduced with all fabricated lies what in fact I am not. I may be presented as a mere servant of a slave country."

Cooperation from America

Wherever Madam Cama went in America, she got complete cooperation from the people there. Due to her policy of hard truthful talking, she had to confront with some difficult situations, but she did not lose heart. Wherever she went, she carried her glorious flag with her.

We can say that she was the first non-government ambassador of India. America and its people appreciated her. She appealed to them for aid for her country. The Americans were stunned at seeing an Indian woman boldly fumes on the stage. It was no little amazement for them to see a woman, standing under her flag, exposing the repression unleashed by the British rule in India.

Addressing the members of the Minerva Club in Woldorf Astoria Hotel, she said:

"The people here are well aware of the circumstances prevailing in Russia, but they little know of the terrible condition that India is suffering at the hands of British government. Our great people are either deported out of the country, or they are lodged in jails, or they are mercilessly beaten and admitted to hospitals. We are peace lovers, we don't want to shed blood, but what we certainly want is that we should educate our countrymen about their rights, so that they can uproot this oppressive rule."

A Successful Traveller

Madam Cama's visit to America had a favourable impact. It resulted into a harmonious relation between Indian revolutionaries and Americans. This was her sole purpose to go to America. She wanted to apprise them of the difficulties being faced by people in India, as well as to guess the attitude of the American officials towards the Indian freedom movement. Describing in her speeches the heartless atrocities being inflicted by the British, she also accepted that they could get back their lost freedom only by following the Russian way.

She continued to send copies of all her newspapers and revolutionary literature to America even after she returned from there, so that the people there could be apprised of the fresh developments and what progress the Indian revolutionary movement had achieved.

The Irish people settled in America offered her specific cooperation. They assured her that they would help her in sending revolutionary literature and explosive materials to India.

Madam Cama assigned the responsibility of all these activities to George Freeman, editor of *Gallic*

American. Freeman showed special interest in the publication of *The Free Hindustan* which was started on the lines of *The Indian Sociologist*.

It was here that Madam Cama met Barkatulla and Phelps. A framework of large number of programmes under her leadership were chalked out in cooperation with them.

She was not keeping well, her diseased body was getting fatigued due to all these hectic activities, yet she was motivated enough as she had succeeded in delivering her message through speeches, interviews and appeals.

There is no written record to show when she returned from America, because she kept visiting one place after another in order to take part in different meetings and conferences.

□

8

In Support of Armed Struggle

Madam Cama and her comrade revolutionaries were now well aware with the view that they could not achieve home rule without an armed struggle.

The Indian community in France accepted Madam Cama as incarnation of goddess Kali; the same goddess who assumes an aggressive and fearsome form, but who remains an affectionate mother for her children.

Madam Cama was the only woman among youth revolutionaries, yet she did not allow her activities to suffer. Every new success motivated her for the next plan. In her newspapers, whether '*Vandemataram*' or '*Madan's Talwar!*', she did not hide herself behind ethics, she adopted the policy of direct war.

An Appeal

In 1908, she published an appeal for all Indians,

titled *'Vandemataram - A Message for Indians'*. This appeal explained her patriotism, the ideals and thoughts of the revolutionaries, as well as why she had supported armed revolution and violent actions. Expressing her views in this regard, she said:

"Countrymen, pay attention to me, I shall not take more than five minutes of your precious time. What I am about to say now, I understand its responsibility well. I am here fully prepared for everything. I have only one life and one incarnation to sacrifice. How can I continue to be silent when I see the massive oppression being inflicted upon our country? Everyday we get information regarding banishment of people from the country. I will put in front of you those methods which appear adequate and justified to me.

"I possess neither power nor rights to tell my patriotic countrymen about these rights, but I will still offer my views. Only the people in India who are being subjected to atrocity; only our people know which path they should choose for themselves.

"I will speak the truth and I am fully confident that all incidents unfolding in India will not have any repercussion on our activities; we will continue to march ahead. Have our countrymen been frightened, have they been terrorized? No, possibly the new rules are worse than the old rules. According to them, the action can be taken, but in fact, it is not very improper.

"Some of you might say that I should oppose violence as I am a woman. Respected gentlemen, I too thought like this until sometime ago. Until three years ago, I could not even talk of violent things, but now the stretching courage and hypocrisy of the moderates have led me to change my views. When the enemy is compelling us to follow the path of violence, why should we criticize it? If we are using force, it is only due to the fact that we are being forced to do so. The English men and women adjudge Sofi Parovanski and his comrades as brave; on the contrary, when the same action is taken by the Indians, they are adjudged criminals. If violence is appreciable in Russia, why is it not so in India?

"Tyranny wherever it might be, tyranny. Repression is repression wherever it might be undertaken. This struggle for freedom needs some exceptions for realizing success. Successful rebellion against the foreign rule is patriotism. What is the meaning of life without freedom? What is the justification of existence without principles? Friends, we all have to set aside all our suspicions, fears, obstacles and doubts, and proceed ahead.

"I appeal to you in the words of Mazzini who said:

'Let us not argue with those who understand what we say but don't abide by it. If our countrymen feel insulted, we should be ready to bring about improvement in their condition, and for this, we should be ready to face any consequences.'

"O Indians! awaken your spirit of self-respect and set down to do your work. Now the days of meetings and resolutions are gone. Just a few foreigners and the English have challenged us. If our millions of countrymen come together to accept this challenge and attack them, is there anything amazing in it? Everybody has to pay the price for freedom. Have you ever seen a country that has attained freedom without paying its price? "Thank Heavens that our countrymen have learnt that it is no less sin to tolerate atrocities. They have learnt how to fight continuously. They have realized that it is better to embrace death fearlessly than to perish like insects. We are now aware of our power. We have now awakened to the name of our ancestors and great country, and oppose all the oppressors.

"The four youths who were mercilessly killed, they have in fact sacrificed themselves on the altar of the motherland. They have sacrificed their lives on the altar of truth, justice and freedom. Today the flag of Vandemataram that I am unfurling before you, has been made by a young patriot; this young man now faces the so-called law court in our country. It appears as if a game is being played in the name of justice and jury; all this is like a cruel joke. We have already witnessed this false show of justice in the cases of Tilak and Pillai.

"Why were they sent to jail? Why were they expelled? Only because they spoke the truth.

"Why this flatterer John Marley sings eulogies of his Western institutions and foreign oak tree?

We don't want any of his foreign institutions. We want our country back. India does not need any foreign oak. We have our own banyan tree and lotus flower. We don't want to follow the English civilization blindly. Sir, our civilization is greater and more esteemed than theirs. What is the civilization of Marley? Oppression of women? For what? For their human rights? In response to their demand of human rights, what all they have been given; nothing but poverty, penury, suffering, robbery and oppression!"

Towards the conclusion of her article, she sent out a touching appeal:

"Indians! Our revolution is sacred. Reason, we should congratulate those Indian men and women who have been struggling against the English atrocities continuously. May their number increase day by day by the grace of God. May their organisations become stronger than before. May the country march ahead towards freedom. May the country witness independence and unity; all these remain my pious wishes. Indian youths, I exhort you to come forward. Friends, march ahead and lead the helpless people of the motherland so that they can be inclined towards true Swaraj. We all have to be righteous.

"We all are for India, and India is for Indians."

In this manner, Madam Cama openly appealed in favour of armed and violent revolution. In her newspaper too, she addressed to the Hindus settled in Europe as follows:

"I will request you in the name of patriotism that you all should take physical training of all types taking advantage of your sojourn in the West. You must know how to shoot, because the day is not far when you will attain your goals of Swaraj and Swadeshi, and when you will have to take up the gun to chase away the English from our beloved country."

□

9

Message for National Integration

Madam Cama and Savarkar had well realized that the moderate Congress would not be able to achieve anything by their petitions. In those days the prevailing circumstances in England were not such in which its people could be presented and convinced of the demand for India's freedom. Therefore, they set out to unite the people of other countries of the world in support of their demand.

The impact of this international propaganda was far-reaching. It did not show its impact immediately, but it increased the number of voluntary members who wanted to adopt the revolutionary methods; and their level of motivation too augmented.

Violence had now been considered mandatory for freedom. It seemed as if the revolutionaries had determined to march ahead like a tempest and root out all obstacles that they might face in their path.

There, Shyamji was being trapped by the English detectives. His newspapers started to be censored. The police raided the press.

Madam Cama had left England and settled in Paris. Now, the name of Madam Cama emerged in Paris and Europe with a new identity. Shyamji and Savarkar continued to work in London, Madam Cama kept visiting there in connection with meetings and conferences etc.

Reference to Secret Report

The secret report, issued by the English government, also referred to the activities being undertaken by Madam Cama. It said that Madam Cama, while addressing revolutionaries in a meeting in the India House on 24 November, 1908, said that they should follow the path of the political assassins of Bengal. The name of each assassin was welcomed by a loud sound of clapping. All of them were motivated to follow on their footsteps and also hoisted a flag.

Demand for Swaraj

In December 1908, a session of the Indian National Congress was organised in the Caxton Hall. In this session, Madam Cama moved the resolution for boycott as well as placed the demand for 'Swaraj' in her speech.

Defining the term 'Swaraj', Veer Savarkar said that it meant complete political freedom of India. This resolution was passed unanimously.

In addition to this, another resolution was moved, in which it was stated that the forthcoming reforms were not likely to benefit India in any way. It also said that those reforms were aimed at creating communal tensions in India.

Birthday of Guru Govind Singh

On 29 December, another meeting was held to celebrate the birthday of Guru Govind Singh. Here too, Savarkar chaired the dais. Addressing the meeting, he said that they should follow the courageous path of struggle by Guru Govind Singh. The meeting approved his statement with a loud clapping. This meeting was also attended by Madam Cama, Vipin Chandra Pal and Lala Lajpat Rai besides Savarkar.

The group photograph of this function can still be seen in the newspaper library of the British Museum. All people in the photograph have their heads covered with a long cloth called '*safa*', and in the background, there is a banner with the words 'Sat Shree Akal', which is flanked by two flags on each side. One of these represented the Sikhism while the other, Indians....

Hindus and Muslims of India

Madam Cama raised different topics in her speeches. She expressed her views on the country's freedom as well as national integration and unity.

We find authentic evidence of this fact from a number of intelligence reports. One such report says that a meeting was held on 20 February, 1909. Its subject was: 'Relation between Hindus and Muslims in India'.

As always, Madam Cama first unfurled the flag on the stage and placed it on the wall. Then she addressed the audience thus:

"...We like the Muslims more than the Hindus because they are strong and fighters; if we have to adopt the path of violence, we would need such people.

"If we do not show our force and violence, freedom will remain only a dream for us. To achieve freedom, failure or success remains in your own hands. If you don't cooperate with the British, the country will be free in no time. Instead working in British subjugation, we should develop our own crafts, industries and trade. All countrymen, whichever faith or community they might belong to, they all will have to strengthen their brotherhood, only then we can achieve the goal of independence...."

□

10

A True Sacrifice

"I admit that I have murdered an Englishman, and I have committed it so that I could protest against inhuman hanging of the patriot young men of India, or sending them to solitary confinement for life, in Cellular Jail in Andaman, called *Kala Pani*.

"I have been guided by my conscience in this endeavour. I could not have fought an open war, so I attacked all of a sudden."

"Being a Hindu, I believe, that a crime against my country is an insult to God. A poor and foolish man like me had not anything but my blood which I could offer to my motherland. This is the reason that I am offering my blood at the altar of my motherland."

"I am showing the path to Indians through my death; and I am proud of my martyrdom. I pray to God that I might be born in the sacred lap of Mother India, so that I could invest myself for the nation if need be. This sequence of birth and sacrifice should continue unless and until Mother India is finally freed."

—Madan Lal Dhingra"

The young revolutionary Madan Lal Dhingra was one of those Indians who had not forgotten their duty towards the motherland despite staying away from India. This boy of a prosperous Khatri family came from the town of Amritsar in India; he was in London for his education. His father and brother were well-known doctors in India. He had been sent to London for education in engineering, but God had written something else in Madan's destiny.

Participation in Conference

Madan found a place to stay in the India House. That place was considered the resort of Indian revolutionaries. It was here that Madan met Savarkar.

The golden jubilee celebration of the 1857 First War of Independence was under way. Invitations were sent to all Indians there stealthily. Madam Cama collected a large sum of money which she deposited in the fund created for assisting the families of the martyrs. All Indians gathered there to offer their tribute to the martyrs. The uprising heroes and femmes were remembered on this occasion. After this, they all swore to sacrifice themselves. Then they deposited the funds to the repository they had collected. In the end of the conference, chapatis were distributed as if they were Prasad (sacred food). Savarkar read out a letter addressed to martyrs titled *O Masters*. This said:

"O martyrs, today is 10th of May. It was on this memorable day in the year 1857 that you waged the First War of Independence in India.

"O Martyrs, the war of 1857 cannot end until revolution dislodges slavery and bondage and adorns freedom on the throne. There is no treaty in the war of revolution, it results into either freedom or death.

"O restless martyrs, fifty years have gone by, but we write out pledge with our blood that we will fulfil your desire by the diamond jubilee. O martyrs, we will take revenge of your blood."

Hearing these words, Madan was also filled with feverishly. The intense feeling of patriotism had subjugated him. The participants in the conference were distributed badges as a mark of remembrance.

Next day, Madan attended his class proudly adorned with the badge on his coat pocket. The English professor asked him to remove the badge. When he refused to do so, the classmates quarrelled and grappled with him. This incident hurt him gravely. Was it a crime to display respect for the nation's martyrs? Was it a crime to remember them and take inspiration from them? Scores of questions clouded his mind.

Friendship with Savarkar

One day Madan expressed his fury before Savarkar. Savarkar was on the mission of propelling a spirit of revolution in the Indian youths. He told Madan that Sir William Hutt Curzon Wyllie was after the Indians, he spied and conspired against them; and it was due to him that the Indian students were disrespected by the British students.

In his heart, Madan vowed to get rid of Curzon Wyllie. When he expressed this desire to Savarkar, he examined this warrior. When he found him true to his word, he promised to support him wholeheartedly.

Towards the Goal

Madanlal left the India House and shifted elsewhere. His friends expressed surprise at this change, but how could they know about the plan going on inside his mind? Madanlal joined a shooting club and started to practise shooting there regularly.

Not only this, he found a pretext to make friends with Sir Curzon Wyllie. He pretended that he was one of those youths who were adorer of the English culture and empire.

Curzon Wyllie felt that he could be the source of secret news from the India House, so he tried to get facts extracted from him. According to the scheme of Savarkar and Madan, only those facts were divulged which would not endanger the secrecy of the India House.

There was an association of the Indians loyal to the British, called 'Indian National Association'. Madan had become member of this association too. He made a plan to assassinate Curzon Wyllie in the annual function of this association.

Vengeance Fulfilled

In the evening, Curzon Wyllie reached at the function of association. Madan reached near Wyllie on some pretence to talk to him, and availing the opportunity, he shot in his chest twice. He also shot him on the face thrice. An Indian Parsi named Kavski Lalkaka rushed to apprehend him, but he too was shot. A number of people surrounded him all of a sudden and took him under arrest. Madan did not hurt anybody else, despite the fact that he still had a loaded revolver and a knife.

The statement that we have put in the beginning of this chapter; was the same that he had kept in his pocket at that time. The police seized it during his search. All patriot Indians were overwhelmed of his courage; however, his father and brother publicly declared to sever all relations with him.

In the court, Madanlal said in clear words that he did not want to hurt Kavaski. But on the second hearing, he stated:

"Whatever I have done was the right thing to do. The English have no right to keep India under their shackles. You can award me death penalty; my death will only contribute to flare up the fire of revolt against the British rule."

This statement of Madanlal was hidden by the police during the initial search. Savarkar possessed one of its copies, which he got published in the newspapers somehow.

Madanlal was infinitely satisfied to know that his voice had reached the public. This historical statement was distributed in each town of India with his picture.

Martyrdom for Motherland

Madanlal Dhingra was sentenced by government to death by hanging. He sacrificed himself for his country on 17 August, 1909. While Madanlal was being hanged in Eatonville Jail in London, Savarkar was at the town square distributing pamphlets.

Pamphlets

The pamphlets had the following statement written on them:

"Today 17 August, 1909 is an important day, the significance of which should be written in blood on the chest of every patriot Indian in bold letters. Madan's soul will guide us all. His pious name will decorate the annals of our history."

This news spread to all European countries. Publishing the picture of Madanlal Dhingra, the newspapers in Ireland wrote: "Ireland pays its tribute to Madanlal Dhingra, who has given up his life for the sake of his country."

Vandemataram

The *Vandemataram*, in its first edition, wrote:

"The immortal Dhingra was a warrior whose devotional words and deeds should be preserved in the hearts over centuries. England thinks that it has killed him, but in fact, he will ever remain alive. He has hurt English sovereignty in India gravely."

Madam Cama could never forget the martyr Dhingra. Following his name, she published a newspaper called *Madan Talwar*. This newspaper, published from Berlin, propagated the revolutionary ideology.

In one of its edition, she wrote:

"The month of August is a period of pious memories. It was in this month that Khudiram Bose bid us farewell first, and it was in the same month on the 17th that Madanlal followed on the footsteps of martyrs and offered himself for sacrifice, and set out for his heavenly abode."

Madam Cama could not forget the martyrdom of Madanlal Dhingra even years later. She loved him like her own son. She had linked all these strangers into a common bond, that was the bond of Mother India. All of them were the sons and daughters of Mother India, who were undergoing many sufferings in the lands away from their motherland, but were still resolved to achieve freedom for their nation.

In 1916, Dr. Bhattacharya met Madam Cama. He has mentioned of this meeting in the book titled *Europiya Bharatiyek Viplaver Sadhana* (*Work for Revolution by European Indians*) in these words:

"Madam Cama's eyes streamed with tears when she remembered Madanlal Dhingra, and she appreciated his incomparable self-sacrifice."

Madanlal was not related to Madam Cama in any way, but he was a son of India; in such a case, the mother of revolution had to have affection for him; it was a spontaneous sentiment on her part.

□

11

For Savarkar

Savarkar's Arrest

In June 1909, Savarkar's brother was imprisoned. He was charged with writing and publishing an inflammatory poem. Savarkar vowed that he would take revenge for this oppression. Of course, Madanlal Dhingra had kept his word by assassinating Curzon Wyllie.

In India, the relatives of Savarkar were repressed. They were trapped in false legal cases and their property was seized. And on the other hand, Madanlal Dhingra had been hanged. The India House, the centre of revolutionaries, too was closed down. There was a time when it witnessed hectic activity in the form of meetings, lectures and discussions under the leadership of Savarkar. Later, the British demolished it completely.

The intelligence personnel were all after Savarkar. His brother had been sentenced to a life term, while Savarkar had to hide himself at one or the other place. It was at this crucial juncture that Madam Cama cared for him and served him like a true mother.

All this while, the case of Browning pistols was in the limelight. Troubled and desperate, Savarkar took refuge in the house of Madam Cama in Paris. After some time, Savarkar decided to go to London. He was advised by his friends against this step; however, he did not pay heed to them. Recalling the friends who had come to see him off in Paris, Savarkar had written:

"Among them I saw two people who looked quiet outwardly, but in fact they were very sad, they were Madam Cama and Hardayal, as if they knew what was in store for me."

The Victoria railway station in London was the site where the police had been deployed everywhere for welcoming Savarkar. There was police force outside the station too. They had been clearly instructed to shoot in case he tried to escape.

The police was very alert in search of this great revolutionary. As soon as the train came to a halt at the platform and passengers started to pour out on the platform, the policemen's sharp eyes were fixed on every Indian youth who stepped out. As soon as Savarkar came out of his third class compartment, he was taken into custody without any questioning; in no time, he was wearing irons. No formality of showing the arrest warrant was fulfilled at this hour.

He was sent to Brimstone jail. London and Indian police officials were elated at this success. The next day newspapers carried the news of his arrest; this made all the revolutionaries anxious.

Plan for Escape

Madam Cama and other revolutionaries knew that if Savarkar was tried in India, it would be a merely outward show. So, they tried their best that Savarkar might not be sent to India. Savarkar was tried in a London court, but it passed the order that Savarkar should be taken to India for further proceedings.

Now the revolutionaries got busy in making several plans to secure his escape. They planned to get Savarkar out of the jail and some other look-alike could replace him; however, this plan did not bear fruit.

Then in conjunction with Irish revolutionaries it was planned that the van, in which Savarkar was to be transported to and from the court, should be attacked enroute and his freedom secured. The plan was final and now preparations were being made; however, on that day, the officials transported Savarkar via another route, due to which the plan could not be accomplished.

Plan for Escape from Maurya

The government was alert at the news filtering in about Savarkar. It took all the precautionary measures to ship him to India by a ship called

Maurya. The voyage commenced with the instruction that the ship would not halt at any port unnecessarily other than for needs concerning oil, coal and essentials.

Under the leadership of Madam Cama and the revolutionary Ayyar, it was planned that Savarkar's release should be secured while the ship was at the French port. Savarkar too was informed of this decision secretly.

When the ship was about to approach France, Savarkar signalled for the natural call. There was a large mirror installed in the toilet so that the guards could keep a watch over him. Savarkar removed his coat and put it on the mirror, and then entered the toilet hole in the wall. When a guard saw the coat hanging on the mirror, he grew suspicious; he peeped into the toilet. He found that Savarkar was about to jump into the sea. He screamed: "Hey, what are you up to? Hold on!"

However, Savarkar swiftly crossed the hurdle and leapt into the sea. The guard broke through the door, while other guards came on the scene.

Savarkar swam to his fullest potential in the saline water, while the policemen kept firing at him. The ship captain put the draw-bridge, from where the policemen fired at him; however, Savarkar was already out of their reach.

Injustice in France

Physical exercise and practice that Savarkar was habituated of, stood by him in times of his need.

At the port, the English policemen ran after him screaming 'Thief, thief!'. Savarkar tried to convince the French troops that he was no thief, rather he was an Indian revolutionary and the English policemen were forcibly trying to arrest him, and they did not have the right to arrest him on the French soil. Savarkar was right to say so, because he was a political prisoner, and he should have got political asylum. This act on the part of English policemen was in clear violation of the international law.

All this while, Madam Cama and Ayyar too arrived on the scene. In fact, when Savarkar jumped into the water, the ship had to accelerate its speed, due to which it arrived at the port before the scheduled time, while Madam Cama and Ayyar had reached the port at the scheduled time to receive Savarkar.

Savarkar had surrendered himself before the French force. Now, the British government had no right to arrest him; however, all laws and regulations were kept aside, he was once again arrested and loaded onto the ship. This was how, Veer Vinayak Damodar Savarkar reached India as a prisoner.

Effort for Savarkar's Release

Savarkar was lodged in Nasik jail. Madam Cama and her comrades were not at all ready to keep silence on this issue. How could the British take away a political refugee forcefully, especially when he had already made to the French soil?

Madam Cama and Lala Hardayal started a movement in France with the help of Jarvis, a socialist leader of France, so that Savarkar's release could be secured. The mayor of Marseilles too enquired into the matter. The French government wanted the British government to return Savarkar to them, but it declined to take any direct action.

The grandson of Karl Marx ran a socialist newspaper in France. Madam Cama wired him this information. He published this news prominently.

Several newspapers in France expressed anguish against the French officials. They emphasised that Savarkar should be released.

Under the mounting pressure from Madam Cama and Lala Hardayal, the international court at the Hague took over the case in its hand, but the British government stuck to its adamant stand.

Sentence to Life Imprisonment

In India, Savarkar was tried for three cases simultaneously. He was charged with the murder of the British officers, and it was also proved that he was an associate of Madanlal Dhingra. He was sentenced to life imprisonment under this charge.

In the second case, it was proved that the pistols by which Mr. Jackson and Mr. Ash had been murdered, were supplied by Savarkar through his cook Chaturbhuj Ameen. Chaturbhuj became a public witness, so it took no time for the court to issue its verdict. This case too culminated into life imprisonment.

Madam Cama hired the services of Vattista, a prominent attorney of Bombay in his defence, yet Savarkar admitted to having sent the pistols, due to which his sentence could not be averted. Listening to the sentence of two life imprisonments, Savarkar laughed:

"I am happy that the British government has sentenced me to life imprisonment twice, and with this verdict, it has approved of the principle of rebirth as enunciated by the Hindus."

The entire property of Savarkar was seized and he was lodged in the Andaman jail, popularly called *Kala Pani*.

Disappointment accruing from Savarkar's case hurt Madam Cama as never before. She had spent much time and money in his deffence, but she never felt sorry about this. Whatever she did was for the sake of her son. She was the mother of revolution, how could she forget about this fact?

Not only this, she kept assisting Savarkar's family even later. Writing about her, Pavlovich writes: "When Madam Cama was working for creating popular opinion for the release of Savarkar from the jail, she little cared for her old age and failing health; she often visited the newspaper offices and requested the journalists to publish materials regarding the release of Savarkar."

□

12

Vandemataram Newspaper

The circumstances had undergone a sea change after the murder of Curzon Wyllie. The British intelligence personnel were already more aggressive. Shyamji Krishna Varma was examined to know if Madanlal Dhingra lived in the India House. The government doubted that he too was involved in Curzon Wyllie's murder.

Perplexed by the pressure, Shyamji sold out the building of the India House. After that, no other place could be arranged where revolutionaries could be lodged. With this, the revolutionaries dispersed and Paris became the new centre for Indian revolutionaries.

Now, Madam Cama was the unanimous leader and Rana became her reliable comrade.

The government unleashed stringent measures to control and prevent revolutionary activities in the form of Explosive Production Law, Indian Penal Code Amendment Act and Press Act etc.

Despite all possible efforts by the British officials, the French officials did not hand over Madam Cama to them. She did not want France to suffer due to her activities, so she chose another place for the publication of her paper.

The publication of the *Vandemataram* started in September 1909. It was edited and printed in Geneva. Later, it was published from Rotterdam.

Lala Hardayal too was in Paris those days. Madam Cama assigned him the responsibility for its editing. It was through this paper that Madam Cama demanded the English to quit India. Her policy was revolutionary in true sense of the term.

In India, the *Vandemataram* newspaper was set up by Bipin Chandra Pal and it was edited by Aurobindo Ghosh. However, it had to be closed down due to the Press Act. It was in the memory of this paper that Madam Cama had named her paper as *Vandemataram*.

The front page of the *Vandemataram* carried two pictures - National Flag of India and Bharat Mata. In the feet of Bharat Mata or Mother India was written the following *shloka* (couplet):

"Atha chetvamimam dharmya sangramya na karishyasi,

Tatah swadharmam kirti cha hitva papabhavapsyati sasi."

(If you do not join the sacred war even after this, it would make you give up the glory of your faith and you will be a sinner.)

Under the national flag was written: A Monthly of Indian Culture.

Further down under was written the lines uttered by Gautam Buddha, which meant:

"So, Anand, become a source of light for yourself. Don't look out for any refuge outside. Get Nirvana [emancipation] by your hard work.

No annual subscription was sought for the *Vandemataram,* therefore, the Indians and revolutionaries subscribed funds for its publication voluntarily. The chief financial burden lay on Madam Cama. The newspaper was delivered all over Europe, and it was slipped into India secretly. This newspaper played a commendable role in evoking the spirit of patriotism in the immigrant Indians.

Even after the Press Act was brought into force, the publication of the *Vandemataram* continued unabated because it lay outside the jurisdiction of the British government. Now, a watch was kept over Madam Cama's correspondence; however, she did not take any time to find other means for her endeavour.

Madam Cama had also published a newspaper in the memory of the eternal martyr Madanlal Dhingra, its name was *Madan Talwar*.

□

13

Daring Madam Cama

Humane Cama

Madam Cama was commendable for her fearlessness and candor. It was quite natural for Madam Cama as a woman to conduct herself in such manner as she was the one who had given up all her worldly pleasures and greed, and had renounced the domestic life voluntarily in order to realize her goals, and this was how she became the mother of revolution. The mother tried to help revolutionaries in every way; she was like a true mother for them. She provided them financial aid and served them when ill; she took upon herself all these responsibilities.

When Savarkar fell ill, she helped him to regain health. When Lala Hardayal faced financial crises, she took upon herself all his responsibility. All these activities showed clearly that she had assumed upon herself the tasks of service which could help in the realization of her goals. She was a true relative of the revolutionaries. Even the closest relatives leave alone in times of calamity, but she was a relative who came more closer during such calamitous times. The entire country was her family. A book titled *Aprakashit Rajnitik Itihas* (Unpublished Political History) by Dr. Bhupendranath Dutta reveals the true image of Madam Cama among the people staying there.

A woman conference was about to be held in Moscow. Mrs. Elwin Roy was responsible for its organisation. She said:

"I have been asked to bring a true Hindu woman; I'll try if I can bring Madam Cama from Paris."

Though Madam Cama could not attend that conference owing to ill-health, yet we can know of the love and respect that she enjoyed in the people's heart.

Daring Madam Cama

Madam Cama was known for her affectionate and humane nature, but sometimes she flowed in the current of her sentiments that she could take greatest risks, which made the people watch her in astonishment. Acharya, her friend, said:

"Madam Cama was like a child who never cared to know what it means to play with the fire. She was a straightforward, natural and explicit woman. She could not only charm others by her speech and writing, but she could hurt and flabbergast others too.

In his Bengali book *Europiya Bharatiyek Viplaver Sadhana* (*Work for Revolution by European Indians*),

Dr. Avinash Chandra Bhattacharya has mentioned one such daring incident:

Rana and Savarkar were her revolutionary comrades. Rana supplied revolvers and pistols to Indian revolutionaries. They all cooperated in such kind of plans.

Those days, Savarkar was an accused in a case of murder in Nasik. During the hearing of the case, something new emerged. In fact, sometime back, Kanhare had murdered Magistrate Jackson by shooting. In 1911, the revolutionary Ayyar shot dead Justice Mr. Eda.

After the investigation of the case, the police arrived at the conclusion that the pistol involved in the murder was sent by Savarkar from London through his cook Chaturbhuj Amin. Those pistols had been bought with the financial aid given by Madam Cama.

Chaturbhuj Amin was taken prisoner. When he could not bear with the terrible torture, he broke down and became a public witness. In this capacity, he gave this statement:

"I had brought these pistols from the residence of Mr. Rana in Paris. This box is his."

When Madam Cama saw Savarkar and Rana being implicated in the case, she was perturbed and became resolute. She never looked back from helping her comrades. So, without seeking any advice from anybody, she made a plan. Let us tell you the fact that those pistols had been concealed by Savarkar and Rana for despatch to Bombay through Amin.

Madam Cama straightway walked in to the office of the British Council in Paris. She sent in her card and wrote a chit: 'To give a clue in the murder of Mr. Jackson and Mr. Esh.'

When the official saw this chit, his joy knew no bounds. He was so easily about to get a clue for the murders in which their enquiry had not made much headway; Madam Cama had come herself for this purpose. He also felt as if Madam Cama wanted to surrender herself.

The officer himself came to the reception to see her. Madam Cama submitted this statement:

"The Browning pistols with which Mr. Jackson and Mr. Esh had been murdered were sent by me to India. This remains true that the box was kept in the house of Sardar Rana, but neither Savarkar nor Rana knew about its contents. It was I who had hidden the guns in the box, so that they could be delivered to India through Chaturbhuj. Both of them are innocent. I am responsible for sending the pistols to India."

Her statement was recorded and she was issued a receipt for this. The copy of Madam Cama's statement was also sent to Bombay public attorney. However, no arrest warrant was issued in her or Ranaji's name. Her statement had been overlooked owing to the international imbroglio that the matter could involve; however, this incident certainly displayed the highest level of her courage, self-sacrifice and enterprise.

□

14

Interest in the Russian Revolution

Madam Cama and her revolutionary comrades were looking for a doctrine to attain their goal. It was during this process that their attention was drawn to the Russian revolutionary movement. Now, Madam Cama took interest in the Russian revolution.

There was an expelled Russian revolutionary, Mikhail Pavlovich, who then lived in Paris. She was in close contact with him. It was he who apprised Madam Cama about the Russian revolution, its goals and socialist ideals.

Madam Cama came to know that the labour class of Europe supported the national freedom movement of India too. Soon, she mixed up with the socialists of France, and joined the Socialist Party. All her study and observation made her to infer that individual efforts could not bear fruit so far as attainment of freedom was concerned; success in this arena could be achieved only through a mass movement or collective efforts. In the beginning, she was attracted towards conventional history of Russia, but later, she was highly impressed by the Russian revolution of 1905.

When she attended the Stuttgart conference in 1907, she appreciated the courageous struggle undertaken by the Russian people.

She said: "We give our good wishes of brotherhood to all those Russian comrades who are engaged in the struggle for liberty."

Pavlovich, a Russian friend of Madam Cama, writes:

"Madam Cama wished to know the role of the worker class in the Russian revolution of 1905, and she read some books on Marxism too.

Despite her advancing age, she remained a firm, vigorous and enthusiastic woman as always; we did not take time in becoming friends."

Madam Cama was a true follower of world brotherhood. The Russian revolution in 1917 roused many expectations in her mind. She wished that India also take inspiration from this. She also realized the value of friendship between Russia and India; she knew of its significance as early as 1907.

Madam Cama, Virendranath Chattopadhyay, Acharya, Shyamji and other revolutionaries had met the Russian revolutionaries who had stood against the Czar. In India too, there was much talk about adopting the methodologies of the Russian revolution, and gradually, people became inclined towards it by consensus.

Madam Cama had understood its need much before, so wherever she lived abroad, she maintained contacts with the Russian revolutionaries. She also rendered all possible help to her comrades in adopting the methodologies of the Russian revolution, so that they can make their country free from the British captivity.

Along with the French and Russian social democrats, she formed a group which was involved in initiating the Indian revolutionaries in political education. All members of this group had a grasp over geography, history, economics, sociology, religion, socialism and communism etc. They were of the view that the entity of the country could be ensured through industrial progress alone. It was said:

"If India does not become free and economically independent like other countries, the wishes of the world's socialists will never be fulfilled."

Contact with Gorky

During the time when Madam Cama was busy reading literature pertaining to the Russian revolution, she met a number of progressive writers too. Maksim Gorky was one of them. He had given a new direction to the society through his writings. His literary talent was unparalleled. On the request of Madam Cama, he sent her the French translation of *The Song of the Falcon*, which motivated her greatly; she commented:

"This is, in fact, far better than any article or declaration."

She maintained her contacts with Maksim Gorky. This writer was also known to other Indian leaders, but his role in the mass movement could be recognized by Madam Cama. Gorky too was a fond of her bravery and patriotism.

Once he requested her: "You should write articles for our Russian magazine *Russian Democracy*. The topics whose theme are 'Indian women and their role in India's freedom struggle'. It would make the Russian women feel grateful to you, to make them aware of how Indian women lived on the banks of the Ganga and followed the exalted ideals of great India's democracy; and how they lived and struggled."

Madam Cama replied: "All my time and energy are devoted to the motherland and the struggle for her freedom. If I find myself capable of writing any such article, I would do it with all my energy."

Madam Cama sent him a few copies of the *Vandemataram* as well as Indian revolutionary literature along with a copy of her photograph. She asked him if he would like to read the book on India's First War of Independence written by Savarkar; she could manage to send it somehow.

This letter and picture of Madam Cama is still preserved in the museum of that great Russian writer.

Severed Contact with Gorky

When Mikhail Pavlovich was returning from Paris after his period of expulsion was over, Madam Cama handed him over a letter for Gorky with the instruction to get it published in Russia. This letter got misplaced somewhere, and after this, Madam Cama could never make contact with Gorky, though she wished to keep contact with him always. Had they continued to be in communication, it would have been certain that many historical documents could have come to the fore.

□

15

An Endless Struggle

Madam Cama lived her life in endless struggle. The age when women enter the maternal happiness and enjoy motherhood, get busy in their households and domestic duties; even in that crucial age, she was busy gathering funds for the revolutionaries. She visited different countries for creating awareness for India's freedom. She was tirelessly roamed for this purpose.

Now, she had lost the company of Savarkar too. On the other hand, the English government was convinced that Madam Cama was involved in propaganda against their imperialist government. At this, the government declared her an absconder and seized her property worth lakhs of rupees. The government realizing this confusion that this could compel Madam Cama to surrender, but it never knew the fabric from which she was made of; but she continued with her activities as before.

The intelligence reports shows that she continued to communicate with the revolutionary comrades in the Cellular Jail in Andaman. She also kept in contact with Acharya and other revolutionaries through telephone or correspondence.

First World War

The First World War started in 1914. With this, Madam Cama became more busy. She convinced Lala Hardayal to work for seeking cooperation of the Turks. The copies of *the Gadar* were being distributed while maintaining contact with the revolutionaries all over the world. Her physique was diseased, but the specialists were unable to diagnose her disease.

In the beginning of the war, the Indian troops were fighting on the European fronts. She also visited the French ports. Those days, Virendranath Chattopadhyay published a newspaper titled *Tagard*. In this newspaper, Madam Cama used to write articles for the troops; she often urged them not to fight for the British, because it was not India's war, rather it was an imperialist war.

One day, she entered the Marseilles cantonment. There she explained to the Indian troops that they should better surrender rather than to fight for the British. They did not need to fight for the very people who had shackled their motherland.

In 1914, as France had joined the allied countries of Britain, it began to put pressure to check the activities of Madam Cama.

Madam Cama was accused that she was involved in conspiracy against the British government while living in France. All her activities were banned by the French government.

An intelligence report reveals that a police prefect had warned Madam Cama to cease her activities as these could result into terrible consequences, so she must stop all her activities. Madam Cama pledged not make any action and sought permission to meet with him that German prisoners of war, but she was not allowed for this.

The British government wanted the French government to banish Madam Cama, but her contact with the Russian comrades bore fruit. Her Russian friends contacted the French socialists and this was how permission was obtained by which she could continue to live in France. She was shifted from Paris and taken to Vichy under house arrest. She lived there for about four years, but her health deteriorated. On the other hand, Rana paid a heavy price for his house arrest. He was imprisoned at an island, where his son and wife died.

Penury and Loneliness

Madam Cama was released at the end of the war; however, her ailment had completely shattered her body. Moreover, she was suffering from penury at this time. She had helped the revolutionaries with money and other things whole life, but now she was suffering herself for lack of money, yet she did not ask anything from anybody for herself. She managed to meet her both ends somehow. However, this scarcity affected her lifestyle greatly; but she was not bit discouraged so far as the spirit of patriotism was concerned; she continued to be a vigorous and enthusiastic worker for the motherland. At times, she tried to organize the team of revolutionaries in Paris.

□

16

My Lovely Country

Whenever we think of the people who have dedicated their lives for the country, the picture of Madam Cama starts to manifest in front of eyes in a fleeting panorama. She continued to raise the flame of freedom abroad for India, she kept motivating and inspiring the youths to work and die for the country; she supported the revolutionaries; she shared their struggle and suffering equally; and she endeavoured to propagate Indianhood all her life; she took all these as the supreme goals of her life. Despite so much of work in these fields, she continued to feel pangs of isolation from her motherland.

This resolute woman, who had been isolated from her family, her relatives, her culture, her land and her country, completely stuck to her resolve of service to the nation; she utilized her expulsion from the country as an opportunity to serve the motherland and get her freed. There is no doubt that she could not have done so much of work, had she been in India, as she had done during her prolonged expulsion of twenty-five years; still, there can be no alternate for the motherland.

Ardent Desire for Motherland

As is said that mother and motherland are greater than heaven even. Madam Cama remained sentimental for her motherland throughout her life. Everything pertaining to her country was like nectar to her – languages of India, news of India, literature of India – everything.

She never hesitated from remarking at the youths who went abroad and got influenced by the Western culture, who overlooked their mother tongue and adopted English in speech, who adopted the Western life style. She had a remarkable command over English as well as a number of Indian languages, yet she never gave up Hindustani. Even on the foreign soil, her soul was always looking for *Naam-e-Jamshed* and *Kaiser-e-Hind*.

These two newspapers were published in Gujarati from Bombay. It was through these that she felt herself connected to her country. If she ever saw an Indian neglecting Indian culture, land or language, she was determined to teach him a lesson.

Instruction to Students

Madam Cama met the Indian students living

there regularly on weekly basis. One day, all students were talking to her in Gujarati. They were then discussing a number of topics including country, international scenario, science, history, culture, art and revolution, and the like. Suddenly she noticed that a student was sitting silently all this while. She asked him: "What is the matter? Don't you find this discussion interesting? Why don't you say something?"

The reply from the student was unprecedented. He said: "I have forgotten Gujarati, so I cannot speak to you in correct Gujarati even if I wish to. If you wish, I can present my ideas in English."

At this, she said: "I feel regret to know that you have forgotten your mother tongue in these eighteen months of your sojourn here; you have forgotten a language which you have been using right since childhood. If your mind is so weak, why have you come here for studies then? Don't waste your parents' money; this education is beyond your capability. I am going to write to your parents to call you back."

Listening to these words, the student was unnerved. He never knew he could get such an extraordinary reply. In no time, he came out of the English influence. Madam Cama's threat reminded him of his mother tongue instantaneously.

Of course, Madam Cama had said these remarks only to make fun of him, but the student assumed that she would actually write to her parents. It is needless to say that after that incident, the student was always found to be talking in Gujarati with his friends.

Love with Own Culture and Civilisation

Madam Cama loved her country more than her life. All countrymen were like her own people. She held her country's culture and life values in a very high esteem. In this connection, once she wrote:

"We don't want the oak tree of England in India, we love our own banyan trees and pretty lotus flowers. We don't have to blindly follow the British civilization. Our own civilization is far better and more liberal than this."

Despite her long stint abroad, Madam Cama remained a true Indian throughout her life.

This revolutionary could never neglect her love for her lovely country even temporarily. However, it is an irony that she could not find solace and happiness in the very soil for which she remained isolated from her family and culture over a long period of time, for which she ran pillar to post in the foreign countries, for which she lived an ordinary middle standard life in an ordinary house, for which she sacrificed all facilities of her wealthy household, for which she made numerous sacrifices. Suffering from incurable ailments, she breathed her last in the hospital. Prior to her return to India, she was made to submit in writing that she would keep away from all types of political programmes, lectures, speeches, functions and literature. You can well imagine how she could have accepted all these conditions by stifling her inner-self, but the conditions forced her to do so. She had to accept all these conditions just to come back to India, her own country. We can estimate the agony that she might have felt at this helplessness.

□

17

In The Lap of Motherland

"I will not return to India, a land of bonded people. I will go there only when it will be free. I have so numerous brave children, and they are doing everything that is possible for them to do. They are sacrificing every particle of their body, every drop of their blood, every moment of their lives. We have to assist them in becoming free."

Harindra Chattopadhyay, in his book *Life and Myself* refers to a meeting with Madam Cama in about 1921, and says:

"Before we departed, we met an important personality. Her name was like a mark of symbol amongst the revolutionaries abroad. She was an old, wrinkled woman; she had large wrists and arms, and her face looked like history of Indian revolution incarnate. Every line drawn on her face expressed a sentence which was written there to manifest her resolve to get India freed. "Once she had said to Harindra Chattopadhyay thus:

"Many people ask me why I don't return to India; they say that I possess intense love for India, still I don't return to India; they wanted to know why I did not want to live in the lap of motherland. These people seldom believe that we can love our motherland even while living abroad. We feel in our hearts every string of pain that our country undergoes. I love the country where I was born and which is alive in my breaths. But listen, I have pledged that I would not return to India on a foreign passport; why should at all I do it?"

Her friends knew how restlessly she wished to return India, still she did not want to go. To find out its cause, one friend asked why don't you return to India.

At this, she said: "I don't return to India because the British government desires that I should beg sorry for all my revolutionary activities, and I should assure them that I would not take part in politics in future."

"Why don't you accept this condition? As a matter of fact, you are already too old to participate in political activities," the friend asked, but he was surprised to hear her answer.

Madam Cama thundered and said: "No, never…I cannot be old for politics at any stage of my life. I still want that I should tour every nook and corner of the country and deliver speeches in political assemblies."

Madam Cama lived in Paris for several decades. Now she had grown old and infirm. She had to undergo a surgery due to a car accident. She also underwent a cataract surgery, after which she suffered from facial paralysis. With the passage of time, she became feeble.

Her old house had been demolished; she now had a poor vision. She had handed over her invaluable flag to Mahadev Rao. Those days, Acharya was with her, who often took her to refreshment centres; it was in these places where she passed a number of evenings in the company of her revolutionary comrades.

Illness and Old Age

People often saw an infirm and feeble old woman walking on the road supported by a youth. Who knew that this was the same Madam Cama who they all knew so well, but now she was under the clutches of advancing age and illnesses.

Madam Cama felt that her last stage was approaching rapidly. Therefore, she bought a place in a graveyard called Pe-la-she. Describing this incident, Acharya says:

"One day she took me to show her grave. She had got the tombstone carved in French and her mother tongue. It was carved with words: *To protest against oppression is abiding by God's wish.*"

Tower of Silence

Madam Cama told him that she had faith in the Zoroastrianism. According to this system, the dead body is offered to the vultures. According to this faith, special emphasis is laid on maintaining purity and piety of natural elements like water, fire and soil. Parsis are of the opinion that a dead body should not be put in these elements and defile them. Therefore, the dead bodies are placed in the Tower of Silence. This is a high tower, surrounded by a high boundary but open from the top. The dead body is eaten away by the meateater birds.

Where these towers were not available for disposing off the dead bodies of the Parsis, there was in vogue a custom to bury the dead bodies. As there was no provision of a Tower of Silence at this place, so she had arranged for a grave for herself.

She said to Acharya: "Our body, in fact, is created by the nature. We have no right over it; therefore, the vultures have every right over it."

Madam Cama: In the Lap of Motherland

After Madam Cama terribly suffered from house arrest and penury, the infirm and old Madam Cama was finally allowed to return to India. When Sardar Singh met her, he was moved at seeing her pitiable condition. The harsh and atrocious British government had allowed her to return only after she signed a memorandum of conditions. She climbed up the ship taking leave of her friends and well-wishers.

She was heading back to India after leading a life in exile for over thirty-five years. The long voyage had made muzzy her already diseased body.

When she set foot in India, she looked at her motherland with great emotions and sentiments. Hurt by old age, her eyes filled with tears, on finding herself in her motherland. When she had left India, she was a young woman, but now she had returned at the age of seventy years, she was old and infirm.

No doubt, she had achieved much in her life. She had invested all her life in realizing the goal of her life; but in some dormant corner of her heart, she must have wished to live the life of an ordinary Indian woman, to share the pleasures and sorrows of her near and dear ones, to celebrate the festivals replete in ancient traditions and customs. Wherever a person may go, he would still wish to return to his roots; these roots are so intense and pleasing that he gets attracted towards them even from across the seven seas.

Madam Cama had now returned to her country, amongst her own people. She was in the company of her friends and well-wishers, but still there existed an impregnable wall of separation with her relatives. Most of the relatives were shying away from a woman who was termed as a dangerous revolutionary.

It appeared as if she had returned to take her last few breaths in India. As soon as she arrived in Bombay, she was admitted in the Parsi General Hospital. Her husband did not approach to see her. Possibly, he had severed all bonds of personal love and acquaintance.

The Fiery revolutionary Madam Cama gave up her life on 16 August, 1936 after about eight-month-long stay in the hospital. No honours were bestowed on her, nor was any condolence meeting held in her memory, nor was there any difference on the world trade owing to her death. She bid farewell to this heartless environment. Maybe the only contentment that she derived was that she was leaving this mortal body in the lap of her motherland and that her body would finally be disposed off according to the Parsi customs.

The body, that had done its duty to remove others' sorrow and grief with a selfless spirit, that had invested itself in the service of the nation, could not resist its desire to do others' good even in its death…indeed this was the body of Madam Cama.

□

18

In Fond Memory of Madam Cama

The freedom of India, for which Madam Cama dedicated all her life, could finally be attained eleven years after her death. Her contribution in the freedom struggle of India can never be overlooked. She was a harbinger of the national movement. Her speeches, articles, appeals and plans were enough to motivate and inspire the mind of the revolutionaries.

In 1910, she addressed the national conference of Egypt, in which only men were participated. Madam Cama believed in equality of men and women. With this belief, she could not keep quite without asking question to the organizers:

"Friends, where is the second half of Egypt? Sons of Egypt, where are your mothers? Where are your sisters? You must not forget that the hands that rock the cradles also build persons, these gentle hands must not be ignored in the course of national life."

She was not wrong to have said so. These were the hands of Madam Cama that had unfurled the national flag at the international stage for the first time. She never desired for any honour, award or appreciation. She was distant from all types of self-adulations by miles, but she could have never hoped that the country would remain ungrateful to her. Can we justify the treatment that we meted out to her? We did not pay our tribute to a great woman on or after her death; the woman who had renounced her family prosperity and comfort; and chose for herself a thorny path so that we might breathe in free air and live proudly amongst the nations of the world.

Birth Centenary

Almost twenty-five years have passed since Madam Cama's death; no one spared a moment to remember her and her contribution. No function was held nor was any memorial raised in her honour. We had placed great ingratitude to forget and neglected her service and contribution to our life.

On the occasion of her birth centenary in 1960, a mass awakening arose regarding her contribution.

Paying obeisance to her at the All-India Women Conference, it was said:

"Madam Cama was one of those early revolutionaries who struggled for freedom. It was due to her nationalist activities that she had to give up her birthplace and household and family to seek refuge in other countries. It was she who gave us our first national flag."

On this occasion, a following proposal too was passed in the Bombay Municipal Corporation, that read:

"The corporation is proud at the historical role of Madam Cama that she played during the early years of the freedom struggle. For the sake of freedom, she underwent expulsion as well as sufferings; But, also became the leading pioneer of inspiration for Indian nationalism. It was she who imagined of a joint Indian republic, with a common language and script. She was the first revolutionary who gave India her national flag, which she first hoisted in the first Socialist Conference in Germany in 1907.

The corporation requests the executive council that, on the occasion of her birth centenary on 24 September, 1961, a suitable main road should be renamed after her in her memory and her achievements."

In Her Fond Memory

In 1962, during the Republic Day celebration, the Maharashtra Secretariat Road was renamed as Madam Bhikaji Cama Road.

A postage stamp was also issued in her fond memory, which had her picture. Her pictures were placed in the Veer Savarkar Halls in Bombay and Pune.

An important area in south Delhi was named after her name as Bhikaji Cama Place.

No doubt, it has been on few occasions and few number of times that we have paid our tribute to this great nationalist woman. We have not remembered even as many times as many years she lived in exile; however, this also remains true that Madam Bhikaji Rustam Cama possesses a special place in our hearts; she was a true patriot, a leading guide in the freedom struggle, a brave and courageous woman, a revolutionary and a lady who possessed a multidimensional personality. The future generations of India will continue to derive inspiration from her for ages to come.

□

Chief Comrades

Madam Cama's stint to overseas remained in the contact of a number of revolutionaries, politicians, leaders and journalists. She cooperated with all of them as much as could be possible; however, she was greatly influenced by Shyamji Krishna Varma and Rana.

In the initial years of her life, she worked as a secretary of Dada Bhai Naoroji. She was doing her tasks wholeheartedly, but when her political horizon expanded, she began to understand the internal conflict of the Congress policies. She felt that the time of submitting petitions was over. She thought why she should bring a solicitation of gaining its freedom? Why should she beg for something which was her own? It must be rightfully hers.

This was how she was disinclined from this 'petition-based' politics. During this stage of ideological transformation, she came into the contact with Shyamji and Rana. These people were rising on the horizon due to their different thinking. Madam Cama had ideological similarity and agreement with these people, so she started to work with them.

Soon, these three emerged as the 'trio' amongst the revolutionaries. This trio successfully carried out a number of plans.

During the course of work under changing circumstances, Shyamji happened to have ideological differences with the other two, but their personal bond never broken. They adopted different paths for themselves, but they all wished to head for the same goal.

While analyzing the entire personality, works and life of Madam Cama, it becomes essential for us to know about these two great personalities; only then we would be able to mark their importance and influence on Madam Cama's life.

SHYAMJI KRISHNA VARMA

Birth and Education

Shyamji Krishna Varma was born on 4 October, 1857 at Mandwa in Kutch province (now in Gujarat). Born in a poor family, Shyamji soon won laurels owing to his brilliant talent. His parents decided that they would certainly educate their son in English.

His mother had died sometime after his birth, following which he shifted to his maternal grandmother where he was admitted to school, as his father lived at another place in connection with business.

Extraordinary talent of Shyamji also impressed Mathuradas Lavaji, and he became his patron. It was owing to his gratitude that now Shyamji could get good quality education. It was due to him that he also learnt Sanskrit. By the age of eighteen years, he was transformed into a fine Sanskrit scholar.

Rich in oriental and western learning, Shyamji was married to a girl belonging to a wealthy and prosperous family. Shyamji was a self-respecting young man, he preferred to earn his livelihood by tuitions rather than seeking help from his rich father-in-law.

He was greatly influenced by Swami Dayananda specifically. His fluent speeches in Sanskrit drew the attention of a large number of people in Nasik, and his family was expanded beyond the Indian borders, even the foreign scholars were keen to know more about him. Shyamji wanted to study abroad in London, but how could he manage so much of money?

Employment and Politics

During his stay abroad, Shyamji got considerable assistance by way of scholarships that he received. He returned to India in 1885 and started his law practice in Bombay. However, the circumstances turned better and he became the Dewan of Ratlam. The ruler and foreign department of Ratlam greatly benefited from his potential. However, one day he took ill during this period and had to resign from the post of the Dewan.

After this, he shifted to Ajmer and started his law practice. He also opened three cotton factories nearby which continued to earn him a large sum of money all his life.

After this, he became the Dewan of Udaipur. In search of better prospects, he went to Junagarh, where the political circumstances were very terrible, replete with conspiracies. In no time, he became a victim of such conspiracies and had to resign from the post of Dewan.

He returned to Udaipur and was appointed the Dewan there; however, the British officers did not want to keep work practices with him, because his opponents in Junagarh had dimmed his image.

Gradually, Shyamji could understand the actual mentality of the British. He came to know that the only purpose of the British was to suppress India and absolute to rule over it anyhow.

Inspiration from Tilak

Lokmanya Bal Gangadhar Tilak raised voice against injustice meted out to Shyamji Krishna Varma, and this was the reason that the two came closer.

In 1907, Tilak revolted in Pune against the British oppressions and atrocities. Now, Shyamji was sure that the British rule could be brought outside only through the use of force.

Mental Conflict

Shyamji Krishna Varma had already

experienced different shades of life. He had seen the working of the princely states as well as the British from close quarters. He also learnt much from great politicians like Tilak; and now he found himself standing at a square from where many great paths went to different directions. He could have become a successful barrister, or a businessman or an extremist political party leader.

Finally, Shyamji decided to work for the country's freedom; but he realized that working under the British rule would amount to just one destination - life imprisonment. So, he thought it was better to go abroad and work for the country's freedom from there.

In this regard, he later wrote in his newspaper: "There is an adage in Sanskrit that it is better not to put your foot in the mud rather than putting the foot in it and then washing it clean. It would be a great perpetration to get yourself arrested by the government and thus get separated from the work you want to do. It would be better to guess such a result in advance and make suitable arrangements so that such a situation does not arise at all."

Follower of Spencer the Philosopher

Shyamji reached London, but he did not become a member of the Congress, because he was a staunch critic of the Congress policies. There he contacted a number of foreign leaders who were fighting for the independence of their respective countries.

He was a follower of Herbart Spencer, so he planned that professors should be appointed to spread the views of Spencer in India, but at this time, Spencer was on his deathbed, so no concrete action could be taken in this regard.

When Spencer died, Shyamji attended his final rites. In the memory of his favourite philosophers, Shyamji instituted six scholarships in the names of Spencer and Swami Dayananda; all these were for Indian students.

Publication of the Indian Sociologist

From January 1905, Shyamji started to publish a newspaper called the *Indian Sociologist*. The newspaper brought out the actual conditions prevailing in India, and said that the suffering of India could be alleviated only after it gets complete freedom. The newspaper started propaganda for the revolutionary policies openly. On 18 February, 1905, Shyamji and a few other Indians came together to establish the Indian Home Rule Society.

Madam Cama too started writing for the newspaper regularly and became a member of the Home Rule Society. Impressed by this success of Shyamji, Tilak wired congratulating him for this feat.

Establishment of the India House

The establishment of the India House was a great and historical step by itself. This house helped the Indian youths living abroad to live together, to transmit their ideas amongst themselves and to focus their energies towards the common goal. Had all of them not got an opportunity to come together under the same roof, there was possibility that the contemporary revolutionary perspective might have been quite different from what had actually developed. Madam Cama too got a field where she could transform her ideas into a concrete form. Nehru himself, in his autobiography, has admitted that the nationalist activities there motivated the Indians living in England.

Severe Blow to British Rule

Once an Anglo-Indian correspondent commented that the idea of home rule did not have any significance in practical politics of India. At this, Shyamji retorted as follows:

"What the British empire has obtained in one day, would be lost in one night.

"There are no white servants, maids, horse-keepers, postmen or policemen in India; you will not find any white employee or shopkeeper in India. If Indians stopped their work just for one week, this empire would crumble like a building of cards, and the whites would be craving even for the food items."

All this while, Shyamji continued to be attached with the contemporary Indian politics through his newspaper and articles. He was accompanied by Rana, Madam Cama, Savarkar, Senapati Bapat and others. The writings of Shyamji had made the foreigners feel that the British rule was not at all adequate for India.

He was firm on his principles too. There arose a number of such opportunities in his life when he gave up everything else but stood with his principles firmly. In his newspaper, he used to publish literature written by patriots and revolutionaries of other countries, so that our countrymen could take inspiration from them.

Whenever a revolutionary occurrence took place in India, his newspaper prominently and promptly gave its reaction. He did not shy away from commenting on the expulsion of Lala Lajpat Rai or the arrest of any revolutionary anywhere in India.

When the activities of the India House surmounted the tolerable limit of the intelligence department, it started to seize Shyamji in different ways.

The newspaper continued to publish aggressive and inciting speeches and articles written by Madam Cama. When it published the translation of *La Marseilles,* it brought about a tempest.

A strange environment had become all around, with the murder of Curzon Wyllie by Madanlal Dhingra. The British newspapers accused him of being involved in this murder. Shyamji was unnerved at this; he only gave a vague statement in this regard. The India House was closed down. His revolutionary comrades were in the favour of a severe action, so they all left for France, and continued to run their revolutionary activities in the way they chose.

Shyamji never indulged himself in any violent activity, but he certainly supported the use of violence for the country's freedom. He never looked back when it came to giving financial aid to revolutionaries.

Final Moment

In 1914, Shyamji moved from France to Geneva, and lived there until his death. Though he happened to have a difference of opinion with Rana a few years ago, yet at the time of his death in 1930, Ranaji made all the arrangements of Shyamji's wealth according to his wish.

Shyamji Krishna Varma played a vital role in providing a revolutionary inclination to the life of Madam Cama; and his influence on her life cannot be negated.

SARDAR SINGH RAO RANA

Birth and Education

Sardar Singh Rao Rana had been born in 1870 at Kantharia village in Kathiawad, Saurashtra (now in Gujarat). His forefathers had been given the title of Rana to recognise their spirit of patriotism, bravery and loyalty. Sardar lived a life of comfort and abundance in his childhood. After he received his education in Rajkot and Bombay, he decided that he would go abroad for higher education.

It was during his term in a Bombay college that the Congress session was held at Pune. He too joined the volunteers. Mr. Banerjee was impressed by his patriotism, politeness and dutifulness. He gave him a copy of his presidential speech, signed by him, and his picture even before he had read out the speech.

Stay Abroad

Rana went abroad in 1898. Those days, the youths of the elite families desired just one thing, that was to do their Bar At Law, so that they could get a prominent administrative position in India. Like in India, Rana continued to adorn his Kathiawadi dress; he declined to wear a western dress despite pressure from his friends. Possibly, he wanted to express his hatred against the British and his pride in his country through this.

Meeting with Shyamji and Naoroji

A storm of patriotism and nationalism was rising in Rana's heart. Soon, he became a point of discussion for all people on this count. It was during this time that he came across Shyamji Krishna Varma. Shyamji possessed a revolutionary ideology, and he had left India to settle there in order to evade his arrest by the British government. Soon, the two became friends. The common goal for both of them was to bring all the Indian youths under the same banner in order to concentrate on their revolutionary activities.

Those days, Dada Bhai Naoroji was the chairman of the Indian Association. This association helped Indians to get their legal rights through legal movements. Rana and Shymaji joined this association, but soon they found that their views and policies were poles apart when matched with those of Dada Bhai Naoroji. They felt that they could not get their rights in alms, they will have to snatch them by whatever means they could adopt, including *Sama-Dama-Danda-Bhed* (the Indian policy of conciliation, bribery, punishment and discrimination to conquer over an enemy).

Consequently, Shyamji and Rana were disinclined away from the association. They wanted to found a separate revolutionary organisation. Ranaji cooperated in publishing a newspaper called the *Indian Sociologist*. Shyamji set up the Home Rule Society, and Rana was deputed as its vice chairman.

The India House and Financial Aid

The India House had been set up in Britain with an aim to protect the Indian youths, who had come to Britain for education, so that they might not become puppets in the British hands. It was a place for the Indians to stay and eat, but in fact, it was a centre of revolutionaries, where the youths were inculcated with revolutionary ideas and trained in revolutionary activities.

There was no scarcity of vigour and vitality for revolutionary activities, but where was the money? It was nowhere in sight. The youths living there had to manage with the limited money they got from India.

Under such a situation, Rana got a fine opportunity to earn money. In July 1900, he went to Paris to see a diamond exhibition. It was there that he came across an Indian merchant, who wanted to make Paris a centre of his trade in diamond, gems and precious stones. He proposed Rana to join him as a partner.

Rana was not interested in this trade, but he joined him as a partner to have necessary money. This was not an improper decision either. In a little time, he earned a great fortune, and he came to be called the 'pearl prince'. With the profit he earned from this trade, he provided financial aid to the revolutionary organisations. He also carried forward a number of revolutionary plans and scholarships on the basis of his profit in this trade.

Supporter of Armed Revolution

Supporting armed revolution, Rana contacted the Russian revolutionaries. When a Bengali revolutionary youth went to Paris for training in bomb-making, Rana gave him shelter to stay as well as helped him in other matters.

Rana also set up a laboratory in his house itself to make bombs. Not only this, he himself got trained in bomb-making along with other revolutionaries.

A booklet was written on bomb-making by a Russian expert. It was translated into English, the copies of which were distributed in different places in India. These booklets were recovered from the houses of a number of revolutionaries during search operations.

Institution of Scholarships

Shyamji Krishna Varma was desirous of having some such determined youths for his revolutionary organization who, at the end of their education, could dedicate themselves to the service of the nation rather than joining the government services. Keeping in view this purpose, he instituted scholarships.

Rana liked this idea greatly. He announced to institute three scholarships in the name of Maharana Pratap, Shivaji and a Muslim ruler. It was on the basis of these scholarships that Lala Hardayal, Veer Savarkar and Senapati Bapat got education in England, and then they rose to be the leading luminaries of the Indian freedom struggle.

Meeting with Madam Cama

It was in Paris itself that Rana met Madam Cama. When she went to Germany to participate in the International Socialist Congress, Rana accompanied her. They continued to work together in revolutionary activities in the years to come. Encouraged by the success of this Congress, Rana and Madam Cama initiated a number of new projects.

Martyrdom of Kanhailal Dutt

In 1908, when the ashes of Kanhailal Dutt arrived in the India House, the Indian revolutionaries decided to hold a programme in the memory of this immortal martyr.

Now, they sat down to discuss who should chair the programme; because they all knew well that anyone who chaired it would become an eyesore for the British government; and possibly he might have to undergo imprisonment. However, Rana proposed his own name for this, and he went on to chair the programme. In it, everybody daubed the ashes of the great martyr on their foreheads and pledged that they would uproot the British from India.

When it became impossible to carry on with political activities owing to strict watch of the intelligence department in Britain, Rana shifted to Paris. By this time, he had also completed his law education.

Rana's Courage

Rana not only supported and aided the newspapers published by Madam Cama, but also made suitable arrangements for supplying arms to Indian revolutionaries. You have already read about the pistol sent by him and how Madam Cama tried to defend them in this connection.

Rana was also involved in getting Savarkar released. He used to find innovative means to send secret revolutionary literature to India. In this connection, the methods adopted by Madam Cama and Rana were worth admiration.

It was owing to these revolutionary activities on their part that they had been declared rebellious. Rana's family members had been warned that they could not correspond with him. The British government was mounting its pressure on the French government to repatriate Rana from France to India; however, Rana never left Paris.

During the First World War in 1914, Rana also contacted the Indian troops deployed in France and urged them to raise their voice against the British government and its atrocities.

The French government could not turn down the request of a friendly nation, so Rana was taken prisoner and was kept in the Borodames Jail. Of course, arrangements were made to secure his release in a few months.

Arrest in Island

Rana was released from the jail, but the government was still terrified from him. He, along with his wife and son, was taken away and kept under house arrest at Martinique island. Rana had to bear the separation from the family too. His nineteen-year-old son Ranjeet could not tolerate the hostile environment at the island, he fell ill and could not last long; his death was a big shock for Rana; and the matter became all the more serious when his wife too breathed her last grieving for her departed son.

When Rana returned to Paris from this island in 1920, he had lost his family.

Re-meeting with Madam Cama

By now Rana's business had been shattered completely; his family had been destroyed; still he felt happy to know that India's freedom struggle had picked up momentum during all these years of his exile. The spirit of nationalism had risen higher and the flame of patriotism was burning more brightly because a number of new leaders had arisen on the horizon.

Rana met Madam Cama, who too had been released from her house arrest; but now, she was an infirm and feeble lady. Under such situations, Rana put in all his efforts to send her back to India. He motivated her to return to India. He had to try for long, only then did the government sanction her return on certain conditions.

Second World War

The Second World War started when Rana was still in exile. He was in Ville those days. He wanted to return to Paris, but the German government put him in the jail. His release could finally be secured in 1941 due to the efforts of Subhash Chandra Bose. After this, he returned to Paris.

Flame of Patriotism

Rana had grown aged now, but his spirit

of patriotism was still strong. He continued to gather Indians in France to observe 13 April as Jallianwala Day and 26 January was also celebrated Kanoply. He had to suffer much after 1945 due to these activities. Remote from his motherland, he willingly and happily underwent torture to remember these days.

Final Period

Rana came back to India on 6 December, 1947 after the country became independent. He felt himself fortunate to stand on the sacred land of independent India. He lived here for a few months, met his old friends and relatives, took part in reception, and returned to Paris in April 1948. Like every true freedom fighter, his heart continued to be anxious for the country's welfare. He said that we would have to take a determined and resolute vow to maintain the freedom got with great difficulty. Sardar Singh Rao Rana died in December 1949 in Paris.

□

An Affectionate Personality

Walk Alone

One of the terrorist 'Trio' of Paris, Madam Cama was a great revolutionary. She was anti-British and undertook all possible activities that she could, in order to dislodge the British government from India. For the British, she was a notorious woman terrorist who was a representation of violent revolution. She was addressed by these epithets owing to her vitality, vigour and aggression, which were intricate parts of her personality. She was called the mother of revolution.

Madam Cama was so furious that even her own relatives did not want to keep any relation with this revolutionary lady. One of her relatives has written in her memoirs that when she (the relative) was about to go abroad, her mother warned her specifically that she should not have anything to do with Cama, nor should she carry any letter or thing for her.

Exiled by her community in this manner, Madam Cama was still determined to proceed towards her goal all alone. The larger image of

Madam Cama was that of a supporter of armed rebellion and bloodshed who kept talking about guns and ammunition; but those who knew her from close quarters said that she was very emotional when it came to her relatives; she was very eager to have letters and pictures from her relatives in India; and she even had tearful eyes when she recalled the flowers in her garden at the backside of her home.

A New Form

The sentimental image of Madam Cama brings to the fore an affectionate personality, who is not inferior to any affectionate motherly woman. She was filled with womanly qualities and traits. When the said relative met Madam Cama, her opinion underwent a sudden change. After her meeting, she wrote:

"Bheeku (Madam Cama) was distantly related to my mother. When my mother introduced to her, she took me in her arms. I used to like that old lady right from the beginning. I never addressed her as Mrs Cama, Madam Cama or Bheeku Auntie; I always addressed her by her first name.

During our meeting, she could not stop herself from remembering her home and family, but she had firmed up her mind, though in her deep heart, she had all those unfulfilled desires which are natural for an exiled heart to have."

Affection with Comrades

Madam Cama was affectionate and warm to all

people, but she was all the more tender and fond of her revolutionary comrades; she considered them all members of the same family. She shared their pleasures and sorrows like her own. She had been separated from her limited family, but now she showered her affection and motherly love on her broader family.

Madam Cama, who inspired people through her speeches, knew well the role of an affectionate and loving mother too; this was the reason that all revolutionaries considered her their mother.

Of course, all of them were undergoing expulsion from their native land; some of them had chosen this exile willingly while others were living abroad out of compulsion; however, Madam Cama was always making effort to resolve all problems that her comrades might face in every aspect of life. She referred to them all as her 'comrades' and 'associates'.

There were occasions when the revolutionaries had some difference of opinion regarding some matter; on such occasions, she would listen to both parties patiently and attentively, and then would find a solution that would satisfy both of them.

Love for Family

Madam Cama was far from her family, but her love for it continued until the very last moment of her life. His wealthy brother Adreshar did not share the parental property with her; he could have done it if he wanted; but Madam Cama never felt bad for this.

It is said that when her brother Adreshar was on his deathbed in Paris, it was none else but she who served him; she never felt for the deprivation. She often said to her friends in an emotional tone: "My brother breathed his last in my lap."

Madam Cama was one of those few people who never felt hurt due to anyone's misbehaviour or disrespect; she always continued to do her duty silently. There is an anecdote about her. She lived for a very long time in a house in Paris; the duration was so long that the house changed hands a number of times. She continued to live in that house as a tenant, while the house-owners continued to change. On one occasion, the new house-owner was an old woman; she was very sweet in talking but could stab at the back if given a chance. She eyed for the finances that Madam Cama received. She often raised the bill amount as and when she saw that Madam Cama had received funds from some source.

When her friends warned her of this unfair practice on part of the old house-owner, and not to trust her, who was out to trick her; Madam Cama said: "I have come to France of my own accord; I have not been invited by the French; so they can charge me any amount they wish. I have forced myself upon them as their guest; therefore, I have no right to complain against them."

Towards Unknown Relations

From the memoirs written by a Parsi lady, Smt. Bani Batlibhai, we can find a religious, womanly, emotional and affectionate image of the revolutionary Madam Cama.

Bani was in a restaurant with her husband and daughter in Ville in 1930. Bani says that an old woman saw them in Parsi traditional saree and approached them, and asked: "Have you come from Bombay?" Then she introduced herself and said that she lived in Paris but was in Ville for a few days.

The old lady hugged them affectionately, which made the Batlibhai family hesitant. At this, the old lady said: "Why are you hesitating? It is in our custom to meet people like this." And then, the old lady invited them to tea at her house.

When Batlibhai family went to see Madam Cama, they carried a bunch of flowers with them. Looking at the flowers, Madam Cama became emotional and her eyes turned moist.

Madam Cama gifted her daughter a pretty border with Chinese embroidery, which was considered very valuable those days. The Batlibhai family preserved this present for a long time in the pleasant memory of that meeting. Years later, they once again met Madam Cama when she was lying ill in the hospital bed.

Madam Cama was proficient in the art of making even the strangers her own. You needed to meet her only once to become her own forever, so charming and affectionate she was.

Savarkar's Heartfelt Sentiments

The way Madam Cama assisted Savarkar and his family is really appreciable. Savarkar considered her as his mother. During the period when Savarkar was in jail, he wrote a few letters to his brother Narain Rao; they are compiled in the book *Andaman Ki Anugunjein* (*Echoes of Andaman*). We shall present a few extracts from this book. When you read these, you will find what type of sentiments Savarkar possessed for Madam Cama:

"Disappearance of your near and dear ones, betrayal by your friends, neglect by your relatives: all these cause to shatter your trust in humanity; but you could get all these back with a single touch of a true, liberal and affectionate hands. How sorrowful it is for me that I could not write a letter to tell this affectionate lady that how greatly I respected her, for her compassion for the needy and her anxiety for the poor. I want to meet her, but it is not possible to do so under the prevailing circumstances. You ought to pay my respects to her in front of all other relatives. She was not related to me, but her help surpassed all limits."

"I have been showered with Madam Cama's affection throughout; her affection cannot be compared with anyone else's affection. She did not forget you even during the war days. We can see that often the blood relations falter, but compassionate people continue to shower their affection."

"My heartfelt respect and love to dear Madam Cama. I earnestly hope that she must be looking after her health well. How grief-stricken I feel at the thought that she has to live a life in exile at a time when she must have been in the company of her smiling children."

□

A Few Extracts from the Paper Vandemataram

Madam Cama knew well that the spirit of patriotism could be propagated by the medium of newspapers. She utilized her iron pen to strike hard at the British government, and she also wrote in detail about all news stories connected with the revolution and revolutionaries, so that the countrymen could become united because of that. Here are a few extracts from the *Vandemataram*:

"The task, that the brave and rational leaders of Bengal have initiated, seems to be impossible to continue in view of the oppressions of the British government; therefore, we will undertake this task through the *Vandemataram*. This task will be accomplished in three phases: to spread awareness among people, to fight a war, and then undertake reconstruction. Any national movement can be accomplished in these three phases; so we too have to pass through these three. History cannot change its course for the sake of India. Mazzini was followed by Garibaldi, who was followed by Kabur. We too have to pass through a similar situation: virtue and reason, war and ultimately freedom."

—September 1909

"The publication of *Madan Talwar* has commenced from Berlin; from the capital of a country which is the greatest adversary of England. We convey our good wishes to our comrades for this selection. The weapons of the British empire would not be able to do any harm in that refuge. Our friendship with the powerful Germany will be quite advantageous for realizing our freedom."

—February 1910

"Young Hindustan, Young Egypt and Ireland, I will republish a booklet titled *How do Russians Prepare for Revolution* for your benefit. I hope that you will like this booklet. Young comrades, I am not for copying anyone blindly, but it is necessary for us to follow different tactics; and only after this, we will be able to choose one matching our attitude and conditions."

—September 1911

Savarkar had been taken under arrest, however, political assassinations continued to take place. When the district magistrate of Mr. Tennivilli, Athe was murdered, the *Vandemataram* stated:

"The message is clear. We have already warned the English that war is inevitable between two of us, and that war has already been started. We are correct to have killed the British. We ought to celebrate whenever a brave patriot kills an Englishman."

—August 1912

Madam Cama appealed:

"Countrymen, write as much as you can. I take all the responsibility. In this newspaper, the name of any writer is not revealed, nor is it published until the writer has consented to it through his signature. All manuscripts will be destroyed before the newspaper is delivered to customers."

—September 1916

In his article, Lala Hardayal wrote:

"Open war against the oppressors will be the ultimate goal of our revolutionary movement. This movement can succeed only when we are supported by the masses and the army. Trust and motivation are the two very important factors for any movement. The problem at present is to bring the army to our side of the fence.

"All educated youths should enroll themselves in the army, and every year trained people should take discharge from it, so that new recruits can be taken. They should be in every battalion and company of the British army, so that we keep getting secret information."

Madam Cama continued to strike hard at the British government with her pen. In an editorial she wrote:

"We should assume that there is no possibility for independent writing and publication of opinions due to the prohibition of the Press Act. Therefore, an important duty of our revolutionary party should be to import revolutionary literature from abroad.

Under such circumstances, the centres for political work should shift from Calcutta, Pune and Lahore to Geneva, London and New York.

We would like to remind our readers that this newspaper is banned in India, yet its copies are being supplied to the homes of our countrymen, and they are being appreciated too. We have already stated that every man and woman connected with the Indian freedom struggle has a pious duty to contribute to propaganda of this type of revolutionary literature. We also entreat our readers to continue to make effort to deliver the future editions of the newspaper in different parts of the country by whatever means that could be available to them."

—January 1911

"With this edition, the *Vandemataram* has entered the third year of its publication. This insignificant servant of the Hindu race would continue to strive like this; and maybe that our writers and publishers change from time to time. I feel happy to state that the newspaper is progressing rapidly; more and more of its copies are being published and distributed."

—September 1911

The writer remarked as under in an article called '*What We Ought to Do*':

"It is Government of India that is chiefly responsible for famine and plague in India. The

Indian revolutionaries can clearly see that this type of atrocities and exploitation can be abolished from India only after the British government is uprooted from India completely and government of the native people is formed. It simply means 'war'. We don't see any other hope to deal with the situation. We will have to reply to this British inhumane treatment in the same coin. Now, it is the need of the hour that we should estimate the real situation and tricks of the enemy."

—February 1912

"We should forget our selfish interests and meanness and recall that Prafulla Chaki, Kanhailal, Khudiram and Madanlal have sacrificed their lives for the sake of our independence. We should keep in mind that Satya Bhama Bai, wife of Tilak, has died due to heart attack just two months back; Indu Bhushan Roy has committed suicide in Andaman because he could not bear the cruel atrocities and torture on him; the wife of Chidambaram has become solitary and helpless. Don't forget that a great number of our comrades are suffering behind the bars. It becomes our moral duty to seek release of Varindra, Savarkar, Hemdas and other revolutionaries from the Cellular Jail in Andaman. Above all, we would not be able to prosper and grow until we are able to drive away the enemy from our motherland."

—September 1912

□

Timeline

1861 – Born on 24 September
1885 – Married to Rustom Cama
1896 – Joined one of the many teams working out of Grant Medical College in an effort to provide care for the famine afflicted people in the Bombay Presidency
1901 – Sent to Britain for medical care.
1905 – Supported the founding of Varma's Indian Home Rule Society together with Naoroji and Singh Rewabhai Rana
1907 – Attended the International Socialist Conference in Stuttgart, Germany
1908 – Came in contact with Shyamji Krishna Varma
1909 – Invited by Lenin to reside in the Soviet Union after the British Government seizure.
1910 – Vehemently supported for gender equality
1914 – Arrested in October when tried to agitate among Punjab Regiment troops during World War I
1917 – Released in November and permitted to return to Bordeaux.

1935 – Remained in exile in Europe till this period

1935 – Arrived in Bombay in November and

1936 – Died at the age of 74, at Parsi General Hospital on 13 August

1962 – The Indian Posts and Telegraphs Department issued a commemorative stamp in her honour

1997 – The Indian Coast Guard commissioned a Priyadarshini-class fast patrol vessel ICGS Bikhaiji Cama after Bikhaiji Cama.

□□□